Wyoming's Ucross Ranch: Its Birds, History, and Natural Environment

Jacqueline L. Canterbury & Paul A. Johnsgard

Zea Books

Lincoln, Nebraska 2019

Abstract

This book profiles 60 of the most abundant, characteristic, and interesting birds that have been regularly reported from the Ucross Ranch and the adjacent Powder River Basin. The 20,000-acre Ucross Ranch lies on the western edge of the Powder River Basin of northeastern Wyoming. Ucross is a textbook example of the prairie grassland/shrubland habitat type referred to as the sagebrush steppe, a landscape that is an icon of Wyoming's vast open spaces.

We focus especially on those species that occur year-round or are present as breeders during the summer months, and we place emphasis on a unique group of sagebrush steppe–adapted birds. We provide information on each profiled species' identification, voice, status, and habitats. "Identification" describes its important visual characteristics (field marks), "voice" provides information on its songs and calls, "status" indicates its relative regional and seasonal abundance, and "habitats and ecology" provides a brief description of its behavior and environmental adaptations. Each species profile also has a calendar of average weekly seasonal occurrence based on long-term regional records.

An introductory essay describes the early history of the Ucross Ranch, which is followed by essays on the natural environment and habitats of the ranch, including the characteristic sagebrush steppe and its associated bird species. The 22,000-word text is supplemented with 60 color bird photographs, a map of the vegetation communities in the Great Plains, and a Bird Checklist of the Ucross Ranch.

Produced in cooperation with the Ucross Foundation and the Bighorn Audubon Society, Sheridan, Wyoming: www.ucrossfoundation.org and www.bighornaudubon.com

ISBN: 978-1-60962-144-5
doi: 10.32873/unl.dc.zea.1071

Composed in Segoe UI types.

Zea Books are published by the University of Nebraska–Lincoln Libraries
Electronic (pdf) edition available online at http://digitalcommons.unl.edu/zeabook/
Print edition available from http://www.lulu.com/spotlight/unlib

Cover photo: Greater Sage-Grouse near Sheridan, Wyoming, by J. Canterbury

Nebraska
UNIVERSITY OF
Lincoln

Raymond Plank 1922–2018

This book is dedicated to the memory of Raymond Plank, who established Ucross Foundation in 1981. His love for Wyoming led to a lifelong commitment to conservation efforts on the 20,000-acre Ucross Ranch, including the planting of thousands of trees and the placement of a conservation easement on the ranch with the Wyoming Chapter of the Nature Conservancy. Plank was a cofounder of Apache Corporation, and Ucross currently leases the ranch to the Apache Foundation, which oversees its operations through holistic resource management. His work also included the restoration of the nineteenth-century ranch house and the barn, known as the Big Red Barn, now listed on the National Registry of Historic Places. Plank was especially fond of the Wild Turkeys at Ucross and kept them well fed through the cold winter months. He also enjoyed watching Turkey Vultures dry their wings while perched on a fence on the hill behind his house. We are all grateful and will miss him.

Contents

Introduction and Acknowledgments

The primary reason this book was written is to give birders and naturalists an opportunity to more easily identify and learn about the birds that might be readily seen at Ucross Ranch and surrounding areas of the Powder River Basin. We have included profiles of 60 of the most abundant, characteristic, and interesting birds that have been regularly reported from Ucross and the adjacent Powder River Basin. We focus especially on those species that occur year-round or are present as breeders during the summer months, and we place emphasis on a unique group of grassland and sagebrush adapted birds.

It was the discovery of early background information about Ucross Ranch that led Jackie Canterbury to decide the area was worth investigating ornithologically. What followed were weekly trips from Sheridan to Ucross to document common and important species in the area. This work was supplemented by the initial work of Nathan Lindsey, who compiled a valuable list of birds beginning in 2007 when he began working at the ranch. These works resulted in the production of a bird checklist in 2018 and the inclusion of the Ucross Ranch as an Important Bird Area (IBA) in 2015.

One of the objectives of this book is to help teach the "average" person how to identify relatively common local species. We provide brief information on each profiled species' identification, voice, status, and habitats. "Identification" describes its important visual characteristics (field marks), "voice" provides information on its songs and calls, "status" indicates its relative regional and seasonal abundance, and "habitats and ecology" gives a brief description of its behavior and environmental adaptations. Each species profile also has a calendar of average weekly seasonal occurrence, based on long-term regional records. However, in the case of seasonal migrants it should be noted that recent global warming trends have substantially modified the migration patterns of temperate-zone species, allowing spring migrants to move northward several weeks earlier than was true historically, and permitting fall migrants to remain in northern latitudes correspondingly longer (Johnsgard, 2009).

We wish to thank Sharon Dynak, president of the Ucross Foundation, and Tracey Kikut, residency manager of the Ucross Foundation, for encouraging the production of this book, and Ruth Salvatore for leading the process for the designation of Ucross as an IBA. We owe a debt of gratitude to Nathan Lindsey for his work on the original vertebrate checklist, his conservation and wildlife management efforts on the ranch, and his willingness to edit this manuscript. We also thank Tina Toth for editing the original manuscript, and Media and Repository Support at the University of Nebraska–Lincoln Libraries. We especially thank and acknowledge Paul Royster, coordinator of the Office of Scholarly Communications and publisher of Zea Books, for seeing our manuscript through to publication, together with the splendid editorial help of Linnea Fredrickson.

The photographs in this book depict wild birds and all were made by the authors, except for additions by Tina Toth of Sheridan and Dave Rinaldo of Scorched Earth Photos, who very kindly allowed their use. The photos' individual copyrights are retained by those individuals who produced them. We also wish to thank the Bighorn Audubon Society for its continual interest and financial support of birds and conservation in the region.

Part I. The Ucross Ranch and Its Birds

Introduction and History of the Ucross Ranch

Sharon Dynak, Ucross Foundation, and Nathan Lindsey, Apache Foundation

The Ucross Ranch is a historic working cattle ranch of 20,000 acres located in northeastern Wyoming. The ranch's name is based on the brand of the Pratt and Ferris Cattle Company of the 1880s, which is a large U with a cross on the right. Colonel James Pratt and Cornelius Ferris were two of the earliest partners, along with Marshall Field of the Chicago department store and a brother-in-law of Colonel Pratt.

Various land transactions were made in the 1890s and later. In the mid-1960s part of the original ranch land was purchased by the Apache Corporation, including properties around Clear Creek that had been part of the original Pratt and Ferris ranch. After that, the ranch was donated to Ucross Foundation, a nonprofit organization. In 1999 Ucross established a conservation easement on 12,000 acres of the ranch, which was held by the Wyoming Chapter of The Nature Conservancy. Ucross has leased the ranch to the Apache Foundation since 2006, and a holistic land management program has been developed, leading to a better understanding of the natural resources of the ranch and its region. This effort has been under the direction of Nathan Lindsey, a biologist who was recently recognized by the Wyoming Game and Fish Department for his conservation and wildlife management work at the Ucross Ranch.

Ucross Foundation was established in 1981 by Raymond Plank, one of the original cofounders of Apache Oil Corporation. The mission of the foundation is to foster the creative spirit of deeply committed artists and groups by providing uninterrupted time, studio space, living accommodations, and the experience of the majestic High Plains while serving as a good steward of its historic 20,000-acre ranch. More than 2,000 artists have spent time in residence at Ucross, many achieving such notable recognition as the Pulitzer Prize, National Book Award, Tony Award, and Academy Award, among many others. In 2018 the foundation established the Ucross Fellowship for Native American Visual Artists. Ucross also operates a public art gallery with rotating exhibitions, open year-round.

In 2011–12 the Ucross Park and Ucross Chapel were created for community use. The Raymond Plank Creative Center was also constructed to serve as a future community resource center and gathering place for retreats and group meetings. Conservation efforts have included the improvement and maintenance of degraded rangelands to highly productive and species-rich environments, resulting in improved habitats for wildlife and fisheries; the planting of thousands of trees; and the provision of educational and outreach opportunities for the general ranchland community. Among such projects are the monitoring of grazing effects on soil, water, and landscape ecology, including rates of soil and stream bank erosion; relative plant productivity; invasive species influences; and other changes in the plant and animal ecosystem structure.

In line with these aspirations of a better understanding of the biotic diversity of the Ucross Ranch, and with the help of wildlife biologist Nathan Lindsey, we have developed a checklist of its documented avian community. As of 2018, the list totals nearly 160 bird species. Among them are several species of special conservation interest, such as the nationally declining sage-dependent Greater Sage-Grouse (Johnsgard, 2002), the prairie-dependent Long-billed Curlew and Upland Sandpiper (Johnsgard, 2001), and a suite of grassland- and sagebrush-adapted birds. Lindsey (2014) also compiled a list of vertebrates of the Ucross Ranch, which includes 149 bird species, 21 mammals (including some generically identified taxa), 9 reptiles, 2 amphibians, and 7 fish.

The Natural Environment and Habitats of the Ucross Ranch

J. Canterbury and P. Johnsgard

The 20,000-acre Ucross Ranch lies on the western edge of the Powder River Basin of northeastern Wyoming and ranges in elevation from 4,000 to 4,600 feet. Ucross is a textbook example of the prairie grassland/shrubland habitat type referred to as the *sagebrush steppe*, a landscape that is an icon of Wyoming's vast open spaces.

The characteristic *sagebrush steppe* habitat type is composed of many native grasses and several sagebrush species, especially big sagebrush. Within the sagebrush steppe exists a patchwork of perennial grasses that are also part of the mixed-grass prairie, which encompasses much of the northeastern corner of Wyoming, including the Ucross

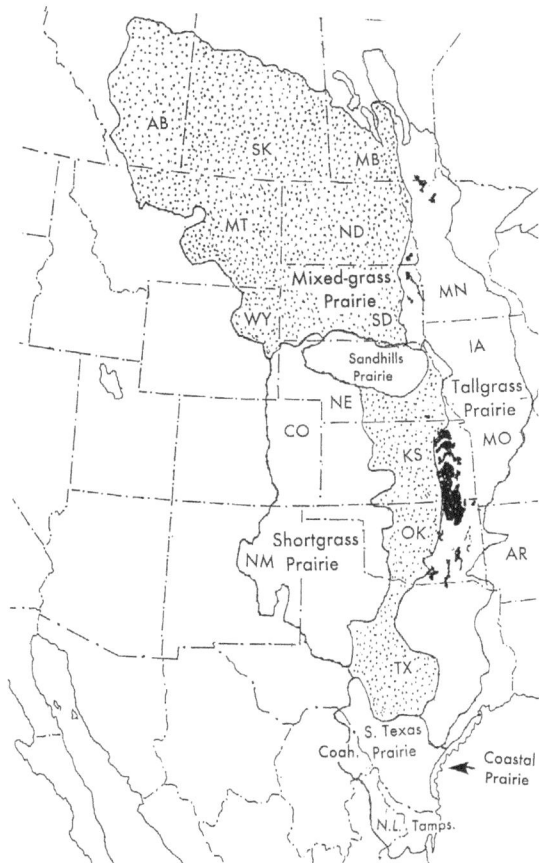

Map. 1. Historic distribution of major vegetation communities in the Great Plains, showing tallgrass prairie (with relic areas of tallgrass shown by inking); the mixed-grass prairie, which extends into the northeastern corner of Wyoming; and the shortgrass prairie along the southeastern border of Wyoming (Johnsgard, 2019).

Ranch (Map 1). This great prairie historically extended from Canada southward through Montana, the Dakotas, and into the northeastern corner of Wyoming, then southward through Nebraska, Kansas, and Oklahoma, finally terminating in Texas. It is largely a result of the Rocky Mountains farther to the west, which block most of the precipitation coming from the Pacific Northwest and in turn cause the moisture to drop on the western slopes of the mountains, creating a drying effect that extends to the eastern plains and beyond. Johnsgard (2005) estimated an overall historic geographic acreage of 140 million acres of mixed-grass prairies in North America and also estimated that about 18 percent remained as of 2000. The northern mixed-grass prairie, which encompasses both North Dakota and South Dakota, is the most important breeding area in North America for waterfowl and is the heart of the breeding range for the continent's grassland birds (Fitzgerald *et al.*, 1999).

Characteristic mixed-grass prairie plants of the Ucross Ranch include needle-and-thread grass (*Stipa comata*), western wheatgrass (*Agropyron smithii*), blue grama (*Bouteloua gracilis*), and Sandberg's bluegrass (*Poa secunda*). Other Ucross grass species of importance are green needle grass (*Stipa viridula*), Idaho fescue (*Festuca idahoensis*), and prairie sandreed (*Calamovilfa longifolia*). Knight (1994) has estimated a mixed-grass plant diversity of 50 or more species per hectare (roughly 2.5 acres). Yet grasslands are not made up of grasses alone but also a significant component of forbs. Forbs, or broad-leaved herbaceous plants, provide important structural diversity and other resources, such as protective nesting cover, seeds, and insects for many grassland-adapted birds (Table 1).

Just as Wyoming has its grasses, so too it has an associated suite of grassland-adapted birds—a small number of evolved and mostly endemic birds that are individually adapted to specific ecological niches. Historically, grasslands in North America were relatively common, yet only 5 percent of all North American avifauna evolved within the Great Plains grassland community (Mengel, 1970). Mengel listed 12 species of birds that he classified as primary grassland endemics, meaning that they are wholly confined to grasslands. He further identified an additional 25 secondary endemic species, which are more geographically and ecologically widespread. Both assemblages evolved within the ecological characteristics of the North American grasslands, including many that coevolved with grazing ungulates (bison and antelope) and prairie dogs (Knopf, 1994). A similar array of 31 Great Plains grassland bird species were identified by Johnsgard (2001).

Six of the 12 primary endemics have been observed at Ucross: Ferruginous Hawk, Long-billed Curlew, Wilson's Phalarope, Lark Bunting, McCown's Longspur, and Chestnut-collared Longspur. Lark Buntings are the most abundant of the primary endemics at Ucross. Nineteen of the 25 secondary species have been documented at Ucross as of 2018. The Western Meadowlark is the most abundant representative of this group. Other documented secondary endemic species include Swainson's Hawk, Northern Harrier, Prairie Falcon, Sharp-tailed

Grouse, Greater Sage-Grouse, Upland Sandpiper, Short-eared Owl, Burrowing Owl, Horned Lark, Sage Thrasher, Western Meadowlark, Dickcissel, Green-tailed Towhee, and five sparrows including the Lark Sparrow, Brewer's sparrow, Grasshopper Sparrow, Vesper Sparrow, and Savannah Sparrow. Of these secondary species, about one-third are part of the sparrow assemblage.

The birds of the grasslands are adapted to a "shifting mosaic" of habitats (Faulkner, 2010). Historically mixed-grass prairies evolved with disturbances such as fire, drought, and grazing by native herbivores, including prairie dogs, bison, and pronghorns (Vickery *et al.*, 1999). Bison and pronghorns ate the grasses and rather rapidly moved on, leaving behind both short and tall grasses, and some ungrazed grasses. Prairie dog activities provided patches of heavily grazed grasses that were very short and sparse. The birds that preferred these short grasses, such as the Ferruginous Hawk and the Chestnut-collared Longspur benefitted. Those species that favored taller grasses, such as the Upland Sandpiper and Dickcissel, used the areas of denser, taller grasses (Dechant *et al.*, 1999, *Upland Sandpiper*; 1999, *Dickcissel*; Table 1). Grassland birds have specific habitat preferences and are adapted to this fluid mosaic of prairie habitats, some preferring short vegetation, others selecting taller, more dense vegetation. The shifting mosaic of habitat types support a myriad of species that are dependent on our prairie grasslands.

Because the North American grasslands have been so altered by humans, the grasslands and their dependent birds have experienced dramatic declines. As a group, grassland-adapted birds have experienced the steepest and most widespread declines of any group in North America. Contributing factors to the decline of grassland birds include conversion for agriculture, unnatural grazing regimes, elimination/reduction of native herbivores, urban development, the introduction and competition of invasive plants, and widespread fire suppression (Vickery *et al.*, 1999). Additional contributing factors include the use of pesticides, eradication of prairie dogs, mowing or plowing of hay fields during the breeding season of prairie birds (April to July), and climate change. As a result of these changes, many of our grassland birds are dependent upon land managers for the re-creation of native habitats. The future of both the grassland birds and native prairies requires a return to land stewardship and to the historical regimes that once shaped a mosaic of unique habitats across the prairie landscape. Ucross has shown itself to be a leader in land stewardship and has adopted many of the latest conservation techniques to protect grasslands and grassland-adapted wildlife.

The characteristic *sagebrush steppe* habitat type is also composed of several species of sage (*Artemisia*), which have diverse plant forms and varied ecological traits. The most common species, big sagebrush (*A. tridentata*), intermixes with semiarid grasslands to form the sagebrush steppe ecosystem (steppe is a Russian word meaning shortgrass prairie). It occurs in semidesert environments of western North America characterized by cold winters and hot, dry summers. There is significant variation in the patch size of sagebrush stands within this enormous ecosystem, which still covers much of Wyoming. For example, sagebrush may occur as a single species or in a mosaic of sages and other shrubs, forbs, and grasses. The entire sagebrush region occupies nearly 155.5 million acres of the Intermountain West, stretching from eastern Washington to Wyoming and south to New Mexico (Paige and Ritter, 1999). Several species of sagebrush (*Artemisia*) inhabit the region from lowlands to subalpine meadows, including big sagebrush. There are 13 different types (species and subspecies) of sagebrush in Wyoming (Knight, 1994); two of them, silver sagebrush (*Artemisia cana*) and Wyoming big sagebrush (*Artemisia t. wyomingensis*), have been found at Ucross. Wyoming has more sagebrush habitat than any other state; estimates range from 23.5 million acres (Knight, 1994) to 37 million acres (Beetle and Johnson, 1982). Whichever of the two estimates is more accurate, the acreage is surely less in 2018 than it was decades earlier.

The sagebrush steppe is important for a myriad of avian species that depend on it for much of their life cycle. About 293 species of birds and 87 species of fish, reptiles, and amphibians are found in sagebrush-associated habitats (Wyoming Interagency Vegetation Committee, 2002). This habitat is critical for birds and other wildlife because it provides nest sites and cover from wind and predators, supports insects for insect-eating birds, and during winter provides a high-protein food source when other plant sources are under snow (Paige and Ritter, 1999). Birds prefer a habitat mosaic that offers diverse patches of open areas as well as stands of dense shrubs,

each with a healthy understory, quite similar in structure to an old-growth forest. At a glance, the understory of the sagebrush steppe seems unimportant, but in fact it is not. For example, sage-adapted birds, like the Greater Sage-Grouse, nest beneath the sage, gaining both shade and overhead visual camouflage. With a careful eye, one can locate flowering plants, which live among a diverse collection of algae, lichen, fungi, mosses, and bacteria (Pitkin and Quattrini, 2010).

Many sagebrush-adapted birds, like the Greater Sage-Grouse, live nowhere else. They are specifically adapted and restricted to sagebrush during the breeding season, or year-round, and are called *sagebrush obligates*. In Wyoming this group includes the grouse as well as the Sage Thrasher, Brewer's Sparrow, and Sage Sparrow (Paige and Ritter, 1999). All the Wyoming sagebrush obligates except the Sage Sparrow have been recorded at Ucross.

Unfortunately, the sagebrush steppe ecosystem is in decline both nationally and in Wyoming, where a sagebrush assessment of the nearby Powder River Basin estimated a 63 percent decrease in sagebrush patch size during the past 40 years (Rowland *et al.*, 2005). That decline does not bode well for sage-adapted species like the Greater Sage-Grouse; the classic "landscape species" of the sagebrush habitat which relies on large blocks of sage-dominated plant communities that occur across the landscape. The bird's numbers have plummeted from millions a century ago to between 200,000 and 500,000 today across its range (US Fish and Wildlife Service, 2015). For northeastern Wyoming specifically, Greater Sage-Grouse numbers have declined significantly, and these declines remain a concern. The Northeast Wyoming Sage-Grouse Plan (Northeast Wyoming Sage-Grouse Working Group, 2014) judged that current decreasing trends are likely a combination of the "cyclic nature of their populations combined with documented influences from wildfires, land conversion, West Nile virus, and energy development in the Powder River Basin." Energy development has created a mosaic of roads, power lines, and human disturbance that has compromised grouse habitats throughout the region. Widespread habitat loss, fragmentation, and invasive nonnative grasses have all compounded the decreasing trends for this species. Future projections will surely add climate change to the list of documented influences on Greater Sage-Grouse numbers as well as on other grassland and sage-adapted species.

When the US Fish and Wildlife Service announced in 2010 that the grouse would be considered for federal listing under the Endangered Species Act, conservation efforts became energized to save the species. A science-based approach for protections that focus on core area habitats began under the leadership of the National Audubon Society's Brian Rutledge. Wyoming is an important part of the conservation effort because the state has 25 percent of the remaining Greater Sage-Grouse habitat, and 37 percent of the remaining birds across the original range of the grouse (US Fish and Wildlife Service, 2015). The good news is that 15 million acres of Greater Sage-Grouse habitat in Wyoming is protected for now, and much of the credit goes to the pioneering and collaborative work of the Audubon Society (Opar, 2015). This pioneering work is currently being challenged by Congress and the Trump administration, and the species has so far been denied federal classification as a Threatened species.

In this area's diverse transitional grassland-sagebrush mix, the breeding birds are likewise a diverse mixture of grassland- and sage-adapted species. Some major and seriously declining grassland-dependent raptors, such as the Prairie Falcon, Swainson's Hawk, Ferruginous Hawk, and Golden Eagle, are keystone predators in the sagebrush steppe ecosystem. The presence of these species, as well as the Burrowing Owl and Short-eared Owl, is evidence of Ucross's healthy and diverse sagebrush steppe community, despite regional and national trends.

Itself a mosaic with its grasslands and sagebrush, the Ucross Ranch is dotted with significant water resources, including riparian areas, wetlands, and ponds. Riparian systems such as Clear Creek and Piney Creek flow through the property and provide one of the most biologically rich environments for birds and wildlife. Although riparian areas represent only about 1 percent of the western United States, they are known to have a remarkably high usage value for wildlife, especially birds (Montgomery, 1996). Rosenberg (2004) estimated that about 50 percent of breeding birds in Wyoming are associated with water in some way and preferentially utilize riparian habitats and wetlands.

Marshes, wetlands, and ponds are also abundant at Ucross. In fact, approximately 100 acres of old river channel wetlands hold water year-round and another 30 acres is in a reservoir. These habitats represent areas where water is present most or all of the time. Wetlands and ponds have vegetation such as emergent cattails, rushes, and sedges that provide important nesting cover and food resources. Whether during migration or the breeding season, these areas support a diversity of species, such as the Sandhill Crane, Red-winged Blackbird, Belted Kingfisher, Osprey, and a variety of ducks and shorebirds.

North American Breeding Bird Surveys from nearby Arvada, performed between 2000 and 2016, indicated that the 15 most common breeding birds of the nearby Powder River Basin, all of which averaged more than 100 reported individuals, were (in order of decreasing abundance) Western Meadowlark, Cliff Swallow, European Starling, Mourning Dove, Western Kingbird, Lark Sparrow, Brewer's Blackbird, Lark Bunting, American Robin, Brown-headed Cowbird, Red-winged Blackbird, Common Grackle, Eastern Kingbird, Bullock's Oriole, and House Wren (Sauer *et al.*, 2017).

Ucross Ranch as an Important Bird Area

In 2015, the Bighorn Audubon Society, in cooperation with Audubon Rockies and the Ucross Foundation, formed a partnership to designate more than 20,000 acres of the Ucross Ranch as an Important Bird Area (IBA). IBAs are identified and designated by the National Audubon Society on the basis of their regional and national importance to a single species or a species assemblage, and are part of a global conservation strategy. This IBA designation recognizes the importance of Ucross for birds nationally and provides a level of support for the many bird species that occupy its diverse prairie grasslands, sagebrush steppe, riverine habitats, wetlands, and ponds.

Status: Relative Bird Abundance and Seasonal Occurrence Terminology

The following terms are used in this book to describe relative bird abundance:

Abundant – Occurs in high numbers during some seasons
Common – Occurs in moderate numbers during some seasons
Uncommon – Expected in low numbers during some seasons
Rare – Occurs only rarely and unpredictably

The following terms are used to describe seasonal occurrence:

Permanent resident – Present year-round, breeding proven or assumed
Summer resident – Breeding in summer is known or likely
Migrant – A seasonal migrant
Winter migrant – Nonbreeding migrant, arriving in fall and departing in spring

Voice: Bird Songs and Calls

Bird song can be defined as a series of complex, often species-specific sounds produced for attracting a mate, announcing a breeding territory, or both. True "songbirds" of the group known as "higher" passerines ("oscines"), a scientific subgroup of the overall group of perching birds (Order Passeriformes), have complex vocal structures (the syrinx and associated muscles) and usually begin learning their song in the nest from parents and nearby neighbors. Young birds then practice those songs (as "sub-songs" or "rehearsed songs") until they are perfected ("crystalized"). As in humans, regional dialects often develop, particularly when birds are geographically isolated, such as in the Bighorn Mountains. Of the world's 10,000 bird species, about half of them technically "sing." Songbirds vocalize using learned or partially learned utterances; even birds like crows and ravens "sing" by this definition. There are also some intermediate groups (the non-oscine passerines), such as kingbirds, phoebes, and other flycatchers, that inherit rather than learn their songs. In many cases they produce simple repetitive calls. Among most birds only males sing, although in some groups (such as phalaropes) the sexual functions are reversed and females establish territories and sing. Song diversity has the advantage of potentially allowing recognition of species, sexes, and individuals, such as pair or family members.

In contrast, bird "calls" are simpler vocalizations that are typically inherited and do not require a learning phase. Because of this, calls are both instinctively produced and understood by all the birds of a particular species. Calls are used for simple but important messages, such as sounding alarm, maintaining pair and family contact, coordinating takeoff and landing, and more.

Birding Ethics and Recommendations

Birds play an important role in all of our natural ecosystems. It is important that we preserve them and their habitats by supporting conservation efforts and by maintaining and protecting both terrestrial and wetland habitats on our properties, including both planted trees and native woodlands. We should also avoid the use of pesticides on our lawns and gardens, keep cats from harming birds, and limit disturbance, especially during the breeding season. Disturbing a protected species' nesting territory can result in unnecessary stress and is a federal offense. Birders should keep an appropriate distance from all birds they observe. The US Migratory Bird Treaty Act of 1918 makes it unlawful "to pursue, hunt, take, capture, kill or sell migratory birds." The statute does not discriminate between live or dead birds and includes all bird parts, including feathers, eggs, and nests, even on private property. Do not use sound recordings to attract birds, as it causes unnecessary stress, especially during the breeding season. When photographing birds, use a telephoto lens and maintain an appropriate distance.

It is also the express wishes of Ucross Foundation that individuals or groups that wish to tour the grounds get permission. Please call 307-737-2291 or email info@ucross.org to schedule an appointment.

Part II. Profiles of 60 Common Birds

Ucross is an incredible place to watch birds. The many planted trees alongside the Big Red Barn (which houses superb art from around the globe), the large cottonwoods standing tall outside the Ucross office, and the confluence of Piney and Clear Creeks, with complimentary benches for bird-watching, all provide a priceless setting. It's not unusual to see raptors in the distance flying gracefully over the grasslands, a Prairie Falcon perched nearby, a Great Horned Owl in the tall spruce tree, warblers flitting through the brush during summer, or resident woodpeckers taking advantage of the large, old cottonwoods that grace the grounds.

For this book, we selected 60 of the most common and interesting birds from the nearly 160 species that have been reported from the area (Canterbury, 2018; Lindsey, 2014).

The species account for each bird provides information on species identification followed by a brief guide for recognizing distinctive songs and calls. The status section provides information on the relative abundance and seasonal occurrence of a species. This is followed by a brief description of the habitats and environmental features that the species prefers. The calendar at the end of each species account shows the species'

documented occurrences for every week of the year at Ucross and can be helpful as a predictive tool for judging the possibility of a species' seasonal presence, both locally and regionally. The "x" refers to recorded occurrences by month and week for the area based on Canterbury *et al.* (2013), Faulkner's guide (2010), 2000–2018 eBird data from Sullivan *et al.* (2009), and Downing (1990). It is important to note that many migrant species may occur outside the seasonal occurrence calendar. Additionally, species that are classified as permanent residents may partially migrate out of a region for part of the year, only to be replaced by same-species migrants from other regions.

Please submit to Bighorn Audubon details of sightings of any species not on the Ucross Ranch checklist. A photograph and written documentation would be appreciated. Email to:
bighornaudubon@gmail.com

Note: In the following profiles, voice descriptions are included only for those species whose vocalizations are significant for field identification. Johnsgard wrote the profiles of the nonpasserines and Canterbury undertook the passerines.

Blue-winged Teal (*Spatula discors*)

Identification: Two Wyoming dabbling ducks, the Blue-winged Teal and the Cinnamon Teal (*Spatula cyanoptera*), exhibit pale blue upper wing-coverts that are easily visible in flying birds and aid greatly in field identification. Males in breeding plumage can be easily distinguished from the less common Cinnamon Teal by the latter's cinnamon-red overall plumage. These "blue-winged" species plus the Northern Shoveler, which has grayish blue upper wing-coverts, make up a group of closely related dabbling ducks. Females of all three are similar in plumage; female Blue-winged Teal have a bill profile that is very slightly shorter than that of female Cinnamon Teal, but otherwise the two are nearly identical. Female Northern Shovelers can easily be distinguished from both by their longer, more spatulate (spoon-shaped) bill.

Voice: Male Blue-winged Teal utter a rather high-pitched *tseel* note in spring but are otherwise silent. Females of both teal species have weak, high-pitched quacking calls.

Status: Common summer resident, wintering to Mexico and Central and South America.

Habitats and Ecology: This species breeds in shallow wetlands with moderate vegetation that are close to grasslands for breeding cover. The birds forage in water or "dabble" with only their bill submerged ("bill-dipping"). Their highest densities are in the mixed-grass prairies of the north-central United States. It is among the latest North American ducks to arrive in Wyoming in spring and the first to migrate south in fall.

JAN	FEB	MAR	APR	MAY	JUNE	JULY	AUG	SEPT	OCT	NOV	DEC
			xxxx	xxxx	xxxx	xxxx	xxxx	xxxx	xxxx	xx	

Northern Shoveler (*Spatula clypeata*)

Identification: This species is the easiest of all dabbling ducks to identify; no other North American duck has a bill that widens toward the tip in a spoon-shaped manner (thus, this bird is often called the "spoonbill duck"). The upper half of the bill also has long plates of comb-like lamellae that are so closely spaced they can filter out tiny invertebrates, providing a unique and easily obtained source of high-protein food. During spring, male Shovelers have iridescent green heads like Mallards, but unlike the Mallards' chestnut breast and grayish white flanks, the Shovelers have chestnut flanks and a white breast. Female Shovelers have a Mallard-like plumage pattern but can be distinguished by their distinctive bill shape.

Voice: Male Shovelers utter low-pitched rattling notes during aquatic courtship but are otherwise silent. The females' calls are Mallard-like but much weaker.

Status: Common summer resident, wintering to southern United States and Central America.

Habitats and Ecology: Shovelers breed on much the same habitat as Blue-winged Teal, namely shallow, often grass-lined marshes rich in aquatic vegetation and associated aquatic invertebrate life, such as insects, insect larvae, small crustaceans, and mollusks as well as tiny plants such as duckweeds. Like other dabbling ducks, the females lay fairly large clutches of about 8–10 eggs that are incubated 24–26 days. Prehatching and posthatching mortality rates are high, and few ducklings survive the five- to six-week fledging period.

JAN	FEB	MAR	APR	MAY	JUNE	JULY	AUG	SEPT	OCT	NOV	DEC
	xxxx	xxxx	xxxx	xxxx	xxxx	xxxx	xxxx	xxxx	xxxx		

Gadwall (*Mareca strepera*)

Identification: Gadwalls are the only dabbling ducks that exhibit a unique white "speculum" pattern on their inner wing feathers, a trait that is usually visible only in flight. At least during spring, male Gadwalls have a distinctively patterned uniformly gray body plumage, except for a black rump and a brownish head. Gadwalls are most often found in shallow marshes, often with American Wigeon, and are easily overlooked because of their rather inconspicuous and dull-colored plumage pattern. Female Gadwalls are most easily identified by their association with males. They are often mistaken for female Mallards but have a grayish bill with yellowish sides rather than a more orange bill with darker markings.

Voice: Gadwalls are most often heard in spring when the males utter their courtship call, a combination of low-pitched *raeb* notes interspersed with *zee* whistles, during aquatic courtship. The female's quacking calls are similar to those of Mallards but are uttered at a higher pitch and more rapidly.

Status: Common summer resident, wintering to the southern United States and coastal Mexico.

Habitats and Ecology: Gadwalls are largely vegetarians and prefer marshes in grassland habitats where aquatic plants grow to or nearly to the water surface. Such plants include wigeon grass, pondweeds, and muskgrass, which they can reach by tipping-up rather than diving. They also prefer grassy nest sites, especially on islands.

JAN	FEB	MAR	APR	MAY	JUNE	JULY	AUG	SEPT	OCT	NOV	DEC
	xxxx	xxxx	xxxx	xxxx	xxxx	xxxx	xxxx	xxxx	xxxx	xxxx	x

American Wigeon (*Mareca americana*)

Identification: The white upper wing-coverts of this dabbling duck are diagnostic but, like the white speculum of the Gadwall, are usually visible only during flight. On the water, the male's white crown and forehead and the somewhat pinkish tones on his breast and flanks are often conspicuous. The female also has a slightly pink tint to her flank feathers and a notably short pink bill with a black tip. The bill is short and narrow, similar to that of a goose.

Voice: Male Wigeons lack quacking voices but repeatedly utter loud double-note whistles during courtship display, often while raising the tips of the folded wings and extending the neck forward. The same whistle is uttered by courting birds while chasing females in flight. Female Wigeons are relatively quiet, even during courtship activities.

Status: Common summer resident, wintering from the southern United States to Mexico and Central America. Small numbers overwinter where open water is available.

Habitats and Ecology: Perhaps more than any other local dabbling duck, Wigeons are highly vegetarian in their diet. They forage not only from the water surface but also along grassy shorelines and even in grassy meadows or in plantings of cultivated leafy crops. Similar to the Gadwall, they prefer open water wetlands more frequently than other dabbling ducks.

JAN	FEB	MAR	APR	MAY	JUNE	JULY	AUG	SEPT	OCT	NOV	DEC
x	x	xxxx	xxxx	xxxx	xxxx	xxxx	xxxx	xxxx	xxxx	xxxx	xxxx

Mallard (*Anas platyrhynchos*)

Identification: This familiar and widely distributed dabbling duck with a green head and narrow white neck ring hardly needs description, but female and late-summer male Mallards are easily confused with other species, unless the bluish speculum, bordered in front and behind with white, can be seen. Males have a chestnut-brown breast, gray underparts, and black rump.

Voice: Male and female calls differ: the common female calls are maternal, while male calls are related to courtship. The most common call is *quack quack quack*.

Status: Abundant permanent resident that can be found wintering as far north as winter allows, as long as there is open water and available food. Often seen in towns and city parks during winter.

Habitats and Ecology: This species prefers aquatic habitats but can nest in variable areas with open water and forage. They also occur in the prairie potholes region. In Wyoming they are common year-round below 8,000 feet (Faulkner, 2010). Mallard success is related to its habitat adaptability, wide food preferences, tolerance of humans, and ability to withstand cold climates. As a result of their adaptability, they are slightly increasing in number and are the most abundant duck species in North America.

JAN	FEB	MAR	APR	MAY	JUNE	JULY	AUG	SEPT	OCT	NOV	DEC
xxxx	xxxx	xxxx	xxxx	xxxx	xxxx	xxxx	xxxx	xxxx	xxxx	xxxx	xxxx

Northern Pintail (*Anas acuta*)

Identification: Northern Pintails have the most streamlined and elegant body form, with the longest neck, most pointed wings, and most elongated tail of any Wyoming duck, traits that are apparent in flying birds. In flight, Pintails also exhibit a uniformly gray underwing pattern, and their upper wings lack the broad white speculum edging and brilliant speculum colors of many dabbling ducks. When standing or swimming, their long necks and breasts, which are white in breeding males, may be seen for hundreds of yards. Female Pintails have subdued brown plumages and grayish bills.

Voice: During spring the fluty courtship whistles of males are uttered, both while swimming and during spirited and dizzying courtship flights above marshes. Like most dabbling ducks, the quacking calls of female Pintails are too soft to be heard at any great distance.

Status: Common summer resident, wintering in the southern United States and Mexico.

Habitats and Ecology: Like the Mallard, Blue-winged Teal, and Gadwall, this is a species closely associated with prairie marshes, although its nests are often placed among sparse vegetation hundreds of yards from the nearest water.

JAN	FEB	MAR	APR	MAY	JUNE	JULY	AUG	SEPT	OCT	NOV	DEC
	xx	xxxx	xxxx	xxxx	xxxx	xxxx	xxxx	xxxx	xxxx	xxxx	x

Common Merganser (*Mergus merganser*)

Identification: Common Mergansers are among the easiest of all Wyoming ducks to identify; in spring the adult males are mostly immaculate white, except for their glossy green head plumage; a long, sloping red bill; and a black back. Females have mostly silvery gray backs and flanks grading into white breast and neck plumage, contrasting sharply with their rufous-brown heads and red bills. In flight both sexes exhibit large white wing patches on the upper wing-coverts and secondary flight feathers.

Voice: Normally almost silent, courting male Common Mergansers utter strange *uig-a* notes reminiscent of the twanging of a guitar string, while females produce harsh *karrr* notes during courtship.

Status: Common permanent resident.

Habitats and Ecology: This large diving duck favors clear-water rivers and nonturbid lakes, where it can see and visually catch fish. The birds swim low in the water, dive easily, and may remain underwater for long periods while foraging. Like other mergansers, this species favors slow-swimming prey rather than swifter and more elusive prey such as trout.

JAN	FEB	MAR	APR	MAY	JUNE	JULY	AUG	SEPT	OCT	NOV	DEC
xxxx	xxxx	xxxx	xxxx	xxxx	xxxx	xxxx	xxxx	xxxx	xxxx	xxxx	xxxx

Ring-necked Pheasant (*Phasianus colchicus*)

Identification: The exotically plumaged male "ring-neck" hardly needs description; it has the longest tail of any North American bird. However, female pheasants might be confused with Sharp-tailed Grouse if their longer tails and more generally mottled brownish plumages are not noted. Pheasants also have very long legs and powerful breast muscles that permit bursts of power, allowing them to flush almost vertically upward, although their flights rarely cover more than a few hundred yards.

Voice: Males utter a distinctive crowing call, a double-noted *caw-cawk*, during late winter and spring that is accompanied by brief wing-flapping and can be heard for more than half a mile. Pheasant calls are highly diverse and have been judged to include up to 24 vocal signals (Giudice and Ratti, 2001).

Status: Common permanent resident. The Ring-necked Pheasant was introduced into the United States from China in the late 1880s and early 1900s.

Habitats and Ecology: Breeding occurs mainly in native grasslands, edges of woodlands and marshes, irrigated agricultural areas, and small patches with tall grass and weedy forbs. Clear Creek Hunting, near the Ucross Ranch, raises pheasants for sport hunting, so this species is relatively common on the ranch grounds.

JAN	FEB	MAR	APR	MAY	JUNE	JULY	AUG	SEPT	OCT	NOV	DEC
xxxx	xxxx	xxxx	xxxx	xxxx	xxxx	xxxx	xxxx	xxxx	xxxx	xxxx	xxxx

Greater Sage-Grouse (*Centrocercus urophasianus*)

Identification: This is the largest grouse in North America (males weigh up to six pounds, females up to three pounds) and is the only Wyoming grouse species directly associated with sagebrush vegetation. Both sexes have long, spikey tails and black abdomens; male Greater Sage-Grouse also have black throats and a small area of bare yellow skin above each eye. In flight both sexes exhibit mostly white underwing patterns, black abdomens, and long, pointed tails.

Voice: Adult males have a large area of white chest and breast feathers that can be erected and expanded by inhalation. During the male's strutting display, air is forced briefly into two patches of bare neck skin ("air sacs") that can be inflated and quickly deflated, producing hollow popping sounds. Simultaneously, a weak *wa-um-poo* vocalization is uttered. A communal strutting location is called a lek, and the birds' collective display activity is called lekking (Johnsgard, 2002).

Status: Common permanent resident.

Habitats and Ecology: Although it is still the nation's largest population of Greater Sage-Grouse, Wyoming's population is declining. The birds are highly dependent on a declining acreage of sagebrush, especially big sagebrush (*Artemisia tridentata*), which is their prime nesting cover and food source. Grouse are residents of the Powder River Basin, and Ucross has a small wintering population.

JAN	FEB	MAR	APR	MAY	JUNE	JULY	AUG	SEPT	OCT	NOV	DEC
xxxx	xxxx	xxxx	xxxx	xxxx	xxxx	xxxx	xxxx	xxxx	xxxx	xxxx	xxxx

Wild Turkey (*Meleagris gallopavo*)

Identification: Wild Turkeys are almost identical to wild-type domestic turkeys but are likely to have tan-tipped rather than white-tipped tail feathers. They are also somewhat lighter in weight (wild-type males weigh up to 16 pounds, females to 9 pounds).

Voice: The familiar *gobble* of male domestic turkeys is the same as that of wild turkeys and can commonly be heard during spring courtship.

Status: Common permanent resident.

Habitats and Ecology: Wild Turkeys were historically native throughout most of the United States but were largely eliminated by hunting. Following extensive reintroduction efforts, the species now occurs in all the contiguous states and parts of southern Canada. The Wyoming population is probably mostly the Merriam's race (*M. g. merriami*), which is primarily associated with open pine savanna and riparian woods. Wild Turkeys are still increasing in both numbers and range; locally, they often interbreed with domestic turkeys.

JAN	FEB	MAR	APR	MAY	JUNE	JULY	AUG	SEPT	OCT	NOV	DEC
xxxx	xxxx	xxxx	xxxx	xxxx	xxxx	xxxx	xxxx	xxxx	xxxx	xxxx	xxxx

Mourning Dove (*Zenaida macroura*)

Identification: Mourning Doves are as familiar to Americans (and as well loved) as apple pie; the doves' summer cooing calls are among the most attractive and nostalgic as any of America's natural sounds. Mourning Doves are mostly gray and black, and are rather dull-colored overall. with only hints of purplish iridescence on the necks of males. However, the small black "beauty marks" on their cheeks reflect an intensely violet glow when viewed under ultraviolet light, suggesting that doves, like many other birds, can perceive ultraviolet and probably use it in social signaling. Their long, pointed tails, most visible when Mourning Doves are in flight, help to distinguish them from the more round-tailed, increasingly widespread and invasive Eurasian Collared-Dove (*Streptopelia decaocto*).

Voice: The familiar cooing of the male is a soothing and sweet-sounding *Oowoo, woo-woo-woo* that is often uttered throughout the entire day.

Status: Common summer resident, wintering variably southward. Mourning Doves have been observed during a few Christmas Bird Counts.

Habitats and Ecology: Mourning Doves breed in a diverse variety of habitats because they are able to nest on the ground, in bushes, or in trees. Furthermore, although doves lay only two eggs per clutch, multiple breedings in a single summer keep their population high. Mourning Doves form loose flocks and migrate varying distances southward in fall. However, with global warming they now tend to winter increasingly farther north, where they are less likely to be hunted for sport.

JAN	FEB	MAR	APR	MAY	JUNE	JULY	AUG	SEPT	OCT	NOV	DEC
	x	xx	xxxx	xxxx	xxxx	xxxx	xxxx	xxxx	xxxx	x	xx

Common Nighthawk (*Chordeiles minor*)

Identification: Common Nighthawks are late spring arrivals, whose presence from late May through late summer is made evident by the periodic loud noises made by displaying males as they dive vertically downward and suddenly pull out, producing a loud percussive sound. In flight, their long wings and the white "windows" near the wingtips are key field marks. Nighthawks spend their daytime hours asleep on horizontal tree branches, flat-topped wooden fence posts, or on bare ground.

Voice: In addition to their display dive and its associated "boom" (caused by air rushing through the wing feathers and vibrating them), male Common Nighthawks often utter a nasal, raspy *peent* call in flight, and females produce a few low clucking notes.

Status: Common summer resident, wintering in Neotropical America. They are one of the last migrants to arrive in Wyoming and one of the first to leave in fall.

Habitats and Ecology: Like swifts and swallows, all species of nighthawks are aerial insectivores, but unlike the others Common Nighthawks forage at dusk, dawn, and even through the night, probably depending on available moonlight to find prey. In towns, the often nest on flat rooftops that are covered with pebbles, but their more typical nest sites are on gravel beaches or barren or burned-over land. Common Nighthawks are no longer common anywhere in North America, as is also sadly true of many other aerial insectivore birds, whose reductions are related in part to rampant use of pesticides.

JAN FEB MAR APR MAY JUNE JULY AUG SEPT OCT NOV DEC
                   xx   xxxx xxxx xxxx xxx

Sandhill Crane (*Antigone canadensis*)

Identification: Sandhill Cranes are easily distinguished from all other local species except perhaps the larger herons; their grayish to rust-brown plumages and the bare red crowns of adults are distinctive, as is their goose-like manner of flying with the neck fully extended.

Voice: Mated pairs maintain their pair bonds with unison calling, which is a series of coordinated calls and distinctive posturing. While unison calling, both birds stand erect with heads thrown back and necks extended. The female utters two higher-pitched calls for each of the male's calls and simultaneously raises her beak to about 45 degrees above horizontal, while the male raises his to the vertical with each single-noted call.

Status: Common summer resident, wintering largely in New Mexico and Texas.

Habitats and Ecology: Sandhill Cranes are associated with wetlands, grasslands, and dense willow thickets along streams and near wetlands, where they often nest in reeds. Their average arrival in this region is March 17. The Rocky Mountain population of Greater Sandhill Cranes breeds throughout parts of Montana, Idaho, Wyoming, Nevada, Utah, and Colorado as well as farther west to the Cascades. About 20,000 birds, or more than 50 percent of the Rocky Mountain population, winter at the Bosque del Apache National Wildlife Refuge in New Mexico (Gerber *et al.*, 2014, Johnsgard, 2015).

JAN	FEB	MAR	APR	MAY	JUNE	JULY	AUG	SEPT	OCT	NOV	DEC
		xx	xxxx	xxxx	xxxx	xxxx	xxxx	xxxx	xxxx	xxxx	

American Avocet (*Recurvirostra americana*)

Identification: Identifying American Avocets is easy—they are the only North American bird species that has a long recurved bill and the only shorebird that is mostly black and white except for a rusty brown head, neck, and breast that turns gray during the nonbreeding season. Avocets are remarkably long-legged, which allows them to wade in fairly deep water and collect tiny food items from the water surface by swinging their head back and forth in a scything motion with the bill held just below the surface.

Voice: A loud *wheet* call is uttered by disturbed birds, often when they are taking flight.

Status: Common summer resident, wintering south to central Mexico.

Habitats and Ecology: Avocets frequent shallow lowland ponds and marshes. They have uniquely recurved bills: the female's is curved more than the male's, but the male's is both longer and straighter (Johnsgard, 1981). These variations could differentially influence the foraging ecology and feeding behavior of the two sexes, allowing for the exploitation of slightly different foraging niches by the pair members, thus reducing intersexual competition for food.

JAN	FEB	MAR	APR	MAY	JUNE	JULY	AUG	SEPT	OCT	NOV	DEC
			xxxx	xxxx	xxxx	xxxx	xxxx	xxxx			

Killdeer (*Charadrius vociferus*)

Identification: The most widespread and common of the North American plovers, the Killdeer is easily recognized by its rusty brown tail and double breast band, together with its incessant calling, especially during the breeding season. Adults feign injury by performing "broken-wing" displays when their nest is threatened, effectively luring most terrestrial intruders away.

Voice: An often-repeated *kill-dee* call, uttered mainly during the breeding season. This call can turn into a loud trill, often given by the feigning bird.

Status: Common summer resident, wintering south to Central Mexico. Small numbers may overwinter, depending upon the weather.

Habitats and Ecology: Killdeer are widely distributed in open landscapes, including roadsides, reservoirs, ponds, gravel pits, golf courses, and suburban lawns, where they feed on earthworms, grasshoppers, beetles, and seeds. Gravelly areas with rocks about the size and color of the birds' eggs are favored. They will sometimes nest on rooftops if gravelly habitats are absent. Killdeer forage visually on surface-dwelling insects while walking about, rather than probing for subsurface foods in the manner of sandpipers and snipes.

JAN	FEB	MAR	APR	MAY	JUNE	JULY	AUG	SEPT	OCT	NOV	DEC
	xxx	xxxx	xxxx	xxxx	xxxx	xxxx	xxxx	xxxx	xx		

Spotted Sandpiper (*Actitis macularius*)

Identification: The Spotted Sandpiper is the most geographically widespread sand-piper in North America. Although it resembles in a general way several other sim-ilar-sized sandpiper species, this bird can be easily recognized by its distinctive teeter-tottering manner of walking. They are usually found close to water, often along streams. When flying, Spotted Sandpipers flap their wings in a distinctively stiff, fluttering manner, which aids in field identification.

Voice: In flight, a series of repeated *weeet* notes is uttered, much like those of some other small sandpipers.

Status: Common summer resident, wintering from the southern United States to southern South America.

Habitats and Ecology: Spotted Sandpipers occupy habitats near water from wild Wy-oming rivers to agricultural ponds, where they forage on invertebrates. The func-tion of the species' teetering walk is uncertain, but it resembles that of the Amer-ican Dipper (*Cinclus mexicanus*). Both species often forage in somewhat noisy aquatic habitats, so perhaps this conspicuous behavior might be a more effec-tive means of long-distance communication than calling.

JAN	FEB	MAR	APR	MAY	JUNE	JULY	AUG	SEPT	OCT	NOV	DEC
			xx	xxxx	xxxx	xxxx	xxxx	xx			

Wilson's Phalarope (*Phalaropus tricolor*)

Identification: Three phalarope species live in North America, and the Wilson's Phalarope is the most terrestrial and the only one that is common at Ucross. All phalaropes swim well and forage while moving quickly and picking up food items from the water surface or just below it. The Wilson's has a uniquely three-colored plumage pattern (white, black, and buffy) on the head and upper neck (thus the name *P. tricolor*), the black becoming brown on the lower neck. Males exhibit the same pattern as females but are less colorful, a reflection of the fact that the external sexual characteristics of phalaropes are reversed, the females being brighter and larger, and taking the initiative in courtship.

Status: A common summer resident, Wilson's Phalaropes winter on saline lakes of the central Andes, after making a 54-hour nonstop flight from the United States (Colwell and Jehl, 1994).

Habitats and Ecology: The Wilson's Phalarope is one of the primary grassland endemics. Their preferred breeding habitats are wetlands, wet meadows, shallow lakes, and ponds that are often associated with grasslands. The sexual reversal of phalarope plumages and sexual behavior is associated with a mating pattern of avian polyandry; the female courts males until she has been inseminated and is able to lay a clutch of fertile eggs. At that time the male takes over incubation and care of the young, freeing the female to pair again and perhaps produce another clutch (Johnsgard, 1981).

JAN	FEB	MAR	APR	MAY	JUNE	JULY	AUG	SEPT	OCT	NOV	DEC
			xx	xxxx	xxxx	xxxx	xxxx	xxx			

Double-crested Cormorant (*Phalacrocorax auritus*)

Identification: Double-crested Cormorants are the only entirely large black water birds at Ucross. In flight they resemble dark geese, often flying in goose-like formation, but they have longer tails, slightly kinked necks, and are totally silent. At close range their orange gular pouches are usually visible. The name "double-crested" is misleading; some short, wispy feather tufts are present on the crowns of both sexes for a few weeks during spring courtship, but they are molted early in the breeding season.

Status: Common summer resident, wintering on the Gulf Coast.

Habitats and Ecology: Cormorants are common on inland lakes, where they dive for fish and invertebrates, and they nest on an island with trees on nearby Lake De Smet. Cormorants are descendants of some of the earliest aquatic birds and were long thought to be close relatives of pelicans. The two differ in many respects, although in both groups all the toes are connected by webbing, which increases swimming and diving efficiency. Cormorants have a highly unusual trait in that their body feathers do not repel water but instead absorb it. As a result, no air is trapped among the water-soaked feathers, and the birds can dive and remain underwater more easily, without having trapped air that would keep them more buoyant (Johnsgard, 1993).

JAN	FEB	MAR	APR	MAY	JUNE	JULY	AUG	SEPT	OCT	NOV	DEC
		xx	xxxx	xxxx	xxxx	xxxx	xxxx	xxxx	xxxx	xxx	

American White Pelican (*Pelecanus erythroryhnchos*)

Identification: Pelicans are unmistakable; the only other pelican species in North America is the coastal Brown Pelican (*Pelecanus occidentalis*). White Pelicans are large and heavy birds. They slightly resemble Snow Geese (*Anser caerulescens*), both having white plumage except for black wingtips, but pelicans fly slower, with slow wingbeats, and hold their head and long beak back resting on their shoulders. Unlike geese they alternate wing-flapping and gliding while in flight and, like cranes and hawks, often use thermal updrafts to gain altitude when flying long distances.

Status: Common summer resident, wintering south to the Gulf Coast.

Habitats and Ecology: All seven pelican species of the world are mainly fish-eaters. Further, all six of the world's white pelicans catch their prey in the same way, by thrusting their beaks into water to catch fish swimming just below the surface, trapping them in their large, expandable gular pouches. White Pelicans often form small groups to drive fish into shallow water, and then simultaneously attack them. In spite of their huge pouches, pelicans have only tiny tongues and seem to lack any sense of taste; thus, they willingly consume dead, rotting fish just as avidly as live ones (Johnsgard, 1993).

JAN	FEB	MAR	APR	MAY	JUNE	JULY	AUG	SEPT	OCT	NOV	DEC
			x	xxxx	xxxx	xxxx	xxxx	xxxx	xxxx		

Great Blue Heron (*Ardea herodias*)

Identification: The Great Blue Heron is the largest common heron of the area and is mostly bluish gray with a black crown-stripe; elongated, very narrow crest plumes; and a tapering yellow bill. Herons fly ponderously, their long legs trailing and the head held back on the shoulders. During summer, breeding herons may be seen perching atop nesting trees beside bulky stick nests; otherwise they are usually found standing in shallow water, searching for aquatic prey that they stab with their dagger-like beaks.

Voice: This heron is mostly silent except during the breeding season when it uses a *roh-roh-roh* call at the nest site and a croaking call when threatened by rival males or other intruders.

Status: Common permanent resident and a regular in small numbers during winter.

Habitats and Ecology: This species occurs along the major riparian areas where there are fish and suitable trees. Large cottonwoods near water are favored locations for nesting colonies, where stick nests are constructed near the crowns. Great Blue Herons tend to preferentially eat fish, but they also prey on frogs and other amphibians. They often remain near their breeding areas until ice begins to form over wetlands, and then they move to where food remains available. A large heronry is located on US Highway 14 west of the Ucross Ranch.

JAN	FEB	MAR	APR	MAY	JUNE	JULY	AUG	SEPT	OCT	NOV	DEC
xxxx	xxxx	xxxx	xxxx	xxxx	xxxx	xxxx	xxxx	xxxx	xxxx	xxxx	xxxx

Turkey Vulture (*Cathartes aura*)

Identification: Usually seen in flight, the Turkey Vulture soars for long periods on wings that are slightly uptilted and two-toned, with black feathers in front and gray behind. Their primaries expose long fingerlike tips while gliding or soaring. The unfeathered head is reddish in adults and appears small relative to the size of the wings and entirely blackish body.

Voice: Because they lack a syrinx, which is the vocal organ responsible for sound, vultures do not vocalize.

Status: A common summer resident, wintering in the southern United States and Mexico.

Habitats and Ecology: The Turkey Vulture is a scavenger species that consumes the carrion of mostly larger animals, such as livestock and deer, which it finds visually as well as by using its remarkable olfactory abilities. Vultures can often be seen soaring above on thermals, using few or no wingbeats. They nest in steep river valleys and place their eggs on bare cliff ledges, under rock overhangs, or in crevices. They can also nest on or near the ground in hollow logs or in large snags, where available. The birds return to the same nest site year after year.

JAN	FEB	MAR	APR	MAY	JUNE	JULY	AUG	SEPT	OCT	NOV	DEC
			xxxx	xxxx	xxxx	xxxx	xxxx	xxxx	x		

Osprey (*Pandion haliaetus*)

Identification: This raptor's white underparts, except for black "wrist marks" on the underside of the wings, are distinctive field marks, as are its long wings, which are usually held at a slightly bent angle rather than horizontally, as eagles do. Ospreys are highly adapted for fish-catching, by snatching them from the water surface while in flight, or by using shallow dives to catch fish that are slightly below the surface.

Voice: The male display call is a high-pitched, slow *chirp*. The threat call, produced when a rival male appears, sounds like a high-pitched whistle.

Status: An uncommon summer resident. Most North American birds winter along the coasts of Mexico, Central America, and South America, although some winter along the west coast of United States.

Habitats and Ecology: Between the end of World War II and the 1970s, Osprey populations crashed because of the use of the synthetic insecticide DDT, which altered hormone levels, reducing eggshell thickness, and preventing hatching. A 1972 federal ban on DDT in the United States was a major factor in the population rebound of Ospreys, Bald Eagles, and many other predatory birds in North America. However, DDT is still in widespread use in Latin America and still affects North American migrant birds that winter in the Neotropics. A successful osprey nesting platform sits 0.5 mile before the entrance to the Ucross Foundation on the right side of Highway 14 coming from Sheridan.

JAN	FEB	MAR	APR	MAY	JUNE	JULY	AUG	SEPT	OCT	NOV	DEC
			xxxx	xxxx	xxxx	xxxx	xxxx	xxxx	xx		

Bald Eagle (*Haliaeetus leucocephalus*)

Identification: Adult birds, with their white heads and tails, are unmistakable, but immature Bald Eagles are mostly brown and best distinguished from golden eagles by their relatively heavy bills and their under wing-coverts, which are paler than their flight feathers. The legs, feet, and beaks of adult Bald Eagles are bright yellow. Young birds become sexually mature and develop adult plumage by five years of age, and by then they have also developed yellow eyes.

Voice: For such a large and powerful bird, male Bald Eagles have a rather timid-sounding call that is a rapid series of high-pitched piping notes. Females often respond with a single call note of similar frequency.

Status: An uncommon summer resident and common overwintering migrant.

Habitats and Ecology: This species feeds locally almost exclusively on carrion, especially road-killed deer, but in many regions it is primarily a fish-eating species. Immature eagles tend to be scavengers until they become proficient predators. During summer, breeding pairs are widely dispersed along rivers and around lakes. Few eagles remain year-round, but some northern migrants spend the winter at Ucross and add to local resident population (Faulkner, 2010).

JAN	FEB	MAR	APR	MAY	JUNE	JULY	AUG	SEPT	OCT	NOV	DEC
xxxx	xxxx	xxxx	xxxx	xxxx	xxxx	xxxx	xxxx	xxxx	xxxx	xxxx	xxxx

Swainson's Hawk (*Buteo swainsoni*)

Identification: The easiest way to recognize Swainson's hawks in flight is to look for their underwing pattern of dark flight feathers (primaries and secondaries) contrasting with lighter under wing-coverts. In nearly all other grassland hawks the flight feathers are not much darker than the under wing-coverts. Perched birds usually exhibit a conspicuous, broad, brown chest-band bounded below with white underparts, and with white on the throat and forehead. Occasionally very dark-plumaged (melanistic) individuals are seen, as also occurs among several other Plains buteos (Johnsgard, 1990).

Voice: When alarmed or disturbed from its nest, this species utters a loud, prolonged scream much like that of the Red-tailed Hawk.

Status: A common summer resident. The Swainson's Hawk is highly migratory, leaving Ucross between late August and mid-September, migrating to southern South America, and returning in mid-April.

Habitats and Ecology: This is a grassland-adapted hawk, tending to replace Red-tailed Hawks in areas where tree-nesting sites are scarce. They are prone to nest in lone trees surrounded by grasslands, whereas Red-tailed Hawks favor nesting in groves of taller trees. At least during late summer the Swainson's Hawk is somewhat insectivorous, often eating large grasshoppers, whereas the other grassland buteos tend to concentrate seasonally on rodents. Like many prairie-dwelling birds, the Swainson's Hawk has been in a long period of population decline (Johnsgard, 2001).

JAN	FEB	MAR	APR	MAY	JUNE	JULY	AUG	SEPT	OCT	NOV	DEC
			xx	xxxx	xxxx	xxxx	xxxx	xxxx	xxx		

Red-tailed Hawk (*Buteo jamaicensis*)

Identification: Red-tailed Hawk plumages are extremely variable with many pattern variations ranging geographically from light to very dark brown or even blackish. The local western race (*calurus*) is relatively dark brown above with extensive brown streaking on the underparts. Very dark plumages are found in some winter migrants (*harlani*). The less common eastern race (*borealis*) is dappled brown and white above and white below, usually with a variably broad belly band of dark splotches. All age groups have dark leading edges on their underwings that extend from the "armpit" to the "wrist," which is the best single identifying characteristic in flight. The rusty tail of adult red-tails is also diagnostic, but first-year immatures have less distinctive brown-banded tails. Red-tailed and other "buteo hawks" (those of the genus *Buteo*) can be distinguished from the less common accipiters (those of the genus *Accipiter*) by their shorter, wider tails and longer, broader wings. Buteos also fly with fairly slow wingbeats and prolonged glides, whereas accipiters alternate quick wing-flaps and short glides.

Voice: A prolonged, descending *keeeer* scream is uttered by alarmed, disturbed, or defensive birds.

Status: Red-tailed Hawks are common residents, winter transients, and migrants at Ucross. Although many breeders migrate to the southern United States for winter, some overwinter locally. Numbers vary seasonally, with local peak migration in early April and October.

Habitats and Ecology: This common buteo hawk occupies a broad range of habitats extending to open country, where nesting often occurs on cliffs. However, trees, especially large cottonwoods and pines, are favored sites where available.

JAN	FEB	MAR	APR	MAY	JUNE	JULY	AUG	SEPT	OCT	NOV	DEC
xxxx	xxxx	xxxx	xxxx	xxxx	xxxx	xxxx	xxxx	xxxx	xxxx	xxxx	xxxx

Rough-legged Hawk (*Buteo lagopus*)

Identification: This large hawk is called "rough-legged" because its tarsal feathers extend down to the base of the toes. Many plumage variations exist between immatures and adults, and in the birds' degree of overall melanism. However, all plumage variants show dark "wrist" patches that are visible on the underwings during flight, and all have white bases to their dark-tipped tails. The breast is often heavily streaked over a buffy background and is bounded behind by a dark belly band. These open-country hawks can often be seen hovering into the wind, a helpful identifying trait that they share with American Kestrels.

Voice: The Rough-legged Hawk is in the region during winter, when it is mostly silent. During the Arctic breeding season, this hawk produces a catlike *mew* call.

Status: A common winter resident, breeding on the Arctic tundra.

Habitats and Ecology: This buteo hunts over open grasslands, meadows, and croplands in winter, all habitats that are similar to its Arctic nesting environment. The birds often perch in wooded riparian areas adjacent to open country. Their populations fluctuate in response to changes in abundance of prey, which is mostly small rodents such as voles and lemmings, on their breeding grounds (Bechard and Swem, 2002).

JAN	FEB	MAR	APR	MAY	JUNE	JULY	AUG	SEPT	OCT	NOV	DEC
xxxx	xxxx	xxxx	xxxx					x	xxxx	xxxx	xxxx

Eastern Screech-Owl (*Megascops asio*)

Identification: Screech-Owls are small, robin-sized, yellow-eyed owls with pointed ear-tufts and a grayish overall plumage that is strongly vertically streaked and barred. This is the only local small owl with ear-tufts. As with other owls, the wings are rounded and the tail is short. The bill is greenish yellow in the eastern species; the Western Screech-Owl (*Megascops kennicottii*) has a blackish bill and is found in southwestern Wyoming.

Voice: The typical eastern species' song is a whinny-like series of rising and falling soft trills uttered by both males and females. They also use a short whinny to defend their territory. These owls can snap their bill mandibles together when agitated, and mated pairs are known to sing to one another during the day and night.

Status: Uncommon permanent resident.

Habitats and Ecology: Associated with riparian cottonwood areas, such as along Little Piney Creek, it prefers large, old trees that provide cavities for nesting, but it can also use nest boxes if provided. They do not excavate their own nest cavities but reuse woodpecker nest holes. Screech-Owls hide in cavities in trees during the day and become active at dusk. They forage on small mammals and birds and sometimes prey on bats. A rufous plumage variant of the eastern species is present in western Nebraska and might rarely occur in eastern Wyoming.

JAN	FEB	MAR	APR	MAY	JUNE	JULY	AUG	SEPT	OCT	NOV	DEC
xxxx	xxxx	xxxx	xxxx	xxxx	xxxx	xxxx	xxxx	xxxx	xxxx	xxxx	xxxx

Great Horned Owl (*Bubo virginianus*)

Identification: With a wingspread of almost four feet, the Great Horned Owl is the largest of the regional owls and locally the commonest. The "horns" of this easily identified owl are ear-tufts that can be fully erected or depressed to the point that they disappear, and they have nothing to do with the owl's hearing. All owls have remarkably large eyes, with round pupils that open widely in the dark to maximize light transmission. The tubular eyes of owls are fixed firmly in their sockets, but the owls' heads can swivel 180 degrees in either direction. This ability allows their frontal parabolic-like facial disks a directional angle that maximizes sound sources reaching their ears, permitting precise stereophonic localization of possible prey. Much hunting is done around dawn and dusk to also allow maximum use of the birds' vision while still exploiting the cover of darkness.

Voice: The usual call is a low five- to six-syllable hoot, *Who-whoah-who, whoah-whoo* (easily remembered as "Don't kill owls! Save owls!").

Status: A common permanent resident.

Habitats and Ecology: A powerful and adaptable owl, this species occurs everywhere from riparian woodlands through the coniferous forest zones, and extends into rocky canyons well away from trees. Nesting sites are thus highly variable but can include abandoned bird or squirrel nests, tree crotches, rock ledges, and rarely even the ground surface. This species nests regularly at Ucross, and birds can often be seen near the buildings.

JAN	FEB	MAR	APR	MAY	JUNE	JULY	AUG	SEPT	OCT	NOV	DEC
xxxx	xxxx	xxxx	xxxx	xxxx	xxxx	xxxx	xxxx	xxxx	xxxx	xxxx	xxxx

Northern Flicker (*Colaptes auratus*)

Identification: This woodpecker is mostly barred brown with black-scalloped pattern-ing, a black breast-band, and underparts spotted heavily with black. A white rump patch is visible in flight. Red malar (moustache) stripes are present in males of the western subspecies (*C. a. cafer*), which also have salmon-red tints on the under-sides of their wing and tail feathers. The eastern subspecies (*C. a. auritus*) is yel-low in tint on these feathers, and males have black malar stripes. Intermediate-colored hybrids often occur where the two races are in contact, particularly east of the Bighorn Mountains.

Voice: Vocalizations include a *wick-a-wick-a-wick-a* uttered on breeding grounds, and a *klee-yer* that is uttered year-round (Wiebe and Moore, 2017).

Status: The Flicker is a common permanent resident, but some seasonal movements from the Rocky Mountains into the Great Plains occur.

Habitats and Ecology: Broadly distributed, Flickers are unusual among woodpeckers because much of their food consists of insects, such as ants and beetles, that are obtained by probing in the ground. Flickers are often found in cottonwoods and riparian zones where snags are present. There they excavate nest holes that later become available for other cavity-nesting species. Flickers can be observed near the Ucross office in the old cottonwoods.

JAN	FEB	MAR	APR	MAY	JUNE	JULY	AUG	SEPT	OCT	NOV	DEC
xxxx	xxxx	xxxx	xxxx	xxxx	xxxx	xxxx	xxxx	xxxx	xxxx	xxxx	xxxx

American Kestrel (*Falco sparverius*)

Identification: About the weight of a Blue Jay, the American Kestrel is the smallest of the North American falcons. All falcons are swift fliers, have notably pointed wings and rapid wing-strokes, and mostly prey on smaller birds that are caught in flight. The American Kestrel is the only falcon species that has rusty brown upperparts and tail, and the only North American falcon that often hovers in the wind while hunting.

Voice: Adults utter shrill *killy, killy, killy* notes when alarmed. Several other falcons have similar alarm calls.

Status: A common summer resident; some birds overwinter during mild years.

Habitats and Ecology: Once called the "Sparrow Hawk," this name is now properly applied only to a similar-sized European species of accipiter that often preys on sparrow-sized birds. American Kestrels have a much more varied diet; they catch and eat a variety of insects, juvenile birds, small rodents, and other vertebrates. However, insects—especially grasshoppers and crickets—are among their favorite foods. Kestrels are cavity nesters, often taking over old woodpecker holes, such as those of Northern Flickers.

JAN	FEB	MAR	APR	MAY	JUNE	JULY	AUG	SEPT	OCT	NOV	DEC
xxxx	xxxx	xxxx	xxxx	xxxx	xxxx	xxxx	xxxx	xxxx	xxxx	xxxx	xxxx

Western Wood-Pewee (*Contopus sordidulus*)

Identification: This inconspicuous brownish flycatcher is much more likely to be heard than seen. If seen, the generally dark grayish brown upperparts without strong wing-barring or a definite pale eye-ring help to identify it. The birds' foraging behavior also helps identify most flycatchers as such because they sally off favorite perches in pursuit of insects and then return to the same perch, a behavior referred to as "sit-and-wait."

Voice: The Tyrannidae family includes pewees, phoebes, and kingbirds, which are not true songbirds and lack their complex vocal structure. Thus they do not produce complex learned songs but instead utter innately inherited calls. In most cases these calls are simple and repetitive. The Wood-Pewee's descending *peeer* and *pzzeeyeer* are uttered during the day and also as the dawn call. The *peeer* call can often be heard from high perches within the male's territory. Identification of Tyrant flycatchers is difficult and often dependent upon learning their unique song patterns.

Status: A common summer resident, wintering in South America.

Habitats and Ecology: Wood-Pewees breed in most coniferous forest types and also to varying extent in aspens, riparian forests, and various open deciduous or mixed woodland habitats. Open forests are favored, especially those dominated by conifers. Nests are built on horizontal branches of trees, or sometimes in a fork, and are usually well covered with spider webs to which lichens may be attached for camouflage.

JAN	FEB	MAR	APR	MAY	JUNE	JULY	AUG	SEPT	OCT	NOV	DEC
				xx	xxxx	xxxx	xxxx	xxxx			

Say's Phoebe (*Sayornis saya*)

Identification: This is a medium-sized flycatcher with a dusky gray-brown back and tinting of rusty brown on the lower breast and belly. The brownish black tail is often pumped up and down. When feeding, the Say's Phoebe usually captures flying insects from a perch, often returning to the same perch. The species can also frequently be seen hover-gleaning insects from the ground.

Voice: The male's primary call is a series of repeated vocalizations: *pit-tsee-eur* and *pit eet*. A *phee-eur* call is commonly used in many situations by both sexes. Males and females have a variable chatter call during breeding, and like other tyrannids they also use a nonvocal "bill snap" to communicate (Schukman and Wolf, 1998).

Status: A common summer resident, wintering from the southwestern United States to central Mexico.

Habitats and Ecology: These birds are found in rather dry habitats, where their brownish earth colors seem especially appropriate. They often occupy canyons, open grasslands, sagebrush, and mountain foothills. Frequently, they nest on human structures. During the breeding season, they often nest under the eaves of the buildings on the Ucross grounds.

JAN	FEB	MAR	APR	MAY	JUNE	JULY	AUG	SEPT	OCT	NOV	DEC
			xxxx	xxxx	xxxx	xxxx	xxxx	xxxx			

Western Kingbird (*Tyrannus verticalis*)

Identification: *Tyrannus* means "tyrant" in Latin and is descriptive of the tyrannids' aggressive defense of a small territory and mate. Kingbirds are commonly seen in summer "hawking"—acrobatically maneuvering from the air to the ground—in search of the insects that make up the bulk of their diet. They are termed the "yellow-bellied kingbird" because of a yellow belly and a pale gray upper breast, black square-cut tail with white on the outer feathers, and brown wings. The bill is short. The range of the similar Cassin's Kingbird overlaps with the Western, and the Cassin's can be distinguished by the darker gray of the head, back, and breast and a contrasting white throat (Gamble and Bergin, 2012).

Voice: Kingbirds, like flycatchers, are not true songbirds, so they do not form complex songs but instead produce simple innate calls. The kingbird produces a *whip* note followed by other high-pitched sounds.

Status: A common summer resident, it winters in southern Mexico and Central America.

Habitats and Ecology: Kingbirds are associated with open areas. Their preferred habitats are open grasslands and sagebrush, but they use trees for nesting and open areas for foraging, often preferring the edges of woodlands or areas where suitable nesting structures are found. They also can be seen in agricultural areas and pastures, where they feed on insects such as beetles, moths, caterpillars, and spiders. Occasionally they eat fruits like hawthorn and elderberry.

JAN	FEB	MAR	APR	MAY	JUNE	JULY	AUG	SEPT	OCT	NOV	DEC
				xxxx	xxxx	xxxx	xxxx	xx			

49

Eastern Kingbird (*Tyrannus tyrannus*)

Identification: The Eastern species' plumage is contrasting black above and white below, with a broad white tail tip that is easily visible in flight. A dark black head often forms a crest, mainly in males. Some say this Kingbird looks as if it is wearing a business suit.

Voice: The dawn call type, sung only by males, is a long series of chits and twitters
like *t't'tzeer*. This Kingbird is one of the noisiest small birds of the region, and from
the time of its arrival until nesting is well underway, its screaming calls and chases
of other birds are often evident. Males and females often call to each other during the breeding season.

Status: A common summer resident, wintering in South America, mainly in the western Amazonian Basin forests where they eat fruit.

Habitats and Ecology: The Eastern Kingbird is associated with open grassland areas
that have scattered trees and shrubs for nesting. This species may also breed in
riparian areas, such as along Piney Creek. The birds select areas where insects
are abundant, catching them in midair and perching on nearby fenceposts while
waiting for their prey. They can also use the wind to their advantage and hover
for insects. Fruits, such as serviceberries and cherries, can be important during
breeding season.

JAN	FEB	MAR	APR	MAY	JUNE	JULY	AUG	SEPT	OCT	NOV	DEC
				xxxx	xxxx	xxxx	xxxx	xx			

Horned Lark (*Eremophila alpestris*)

Identification: This small grassland species has feathered "horns," which are visible only at close range and can be raised or lowered. The white-edged black tail and brown nape, back, and rump coloration are most useful as field marks, as is the black breast-band. The brown back coloration varies geographically, with lighter shades occurring in the drier areas of western North America; the coloration is thought to be related to the color of local soils (Beason, 1995).

Voice: In spring, males sing an extended flight song above their territory that is a high-pitched assortment of tinkling notes. The *su-weet* note is most common. They also deliver a song from the ground and from the ground and perches.

Status: A common permanent resident.

Habitats and Ecology: A common bird of open country and a secondary endemic species, Horned Larks prefer sparsely vegetated grasslands and agricultural fields with bare ground to grasses taller than a few centimeters. The birds have an enormous ecological and geographic range in North America; the northernmost populations are migratory, moving variably south in winter (Beason, 1995).

JAN	FEB	MAR	APR	MAY	JUNE	JULY	AUG	SEPT	OCT	NOV	DEC
xxxx	xxxx	xxxx	xxxx	xxxx	xxxx	xxxx	xxxx	xxxx	xxxx	xxxx	xxxx

Tree Swallow (*Tachycineta bicolor*)

Identification: This attractive swallow is a two-toned iridescent bluish black above and immaculate white below, and has a somewhat forked tail. It closely resembles the Violet-green Swallow but lacks that western species' large white flank patches.

Voice: Both males and females of this species sing a high-pitched and liquid *chirp* and *gurgle*. Their calls, similar to their songs, are a series of chirps but also include ticking sounds and chatters.

Status: A common summer resident, wintering in Mexico and Central America. It is the earliest local swallow to return north in spring to its breeding grounds.

Habitats and Ecology: Breeding in the region extends from riparian woodlands through the aspen zone and into a variety of open habitats like fields and wetlands. Outside of the breeding season they are seen over lakes and rivers, where they frequently form huge flocks. Nesting is common in aspen groves, where old woodpecker holes are available, but they also nest in birdhouses. At times a male may support two mates at separate nest sites, and reportedly even three birds may build a nest, incubate eggs, and raise the young.

JAN	FEB	MAR	APR	MAY	JUNE	JULY	AUG	SEPT	OCT	NOV	DEC
		x	xxxx	xxxx	xxxx	xxxx	xxxx	xx			

Cliff Swallow (*Petrochelidon pyrrhonota*)

Identification: This swallow is easily recognized by its golden-orange rump patch, its square tail rather than forked (as the Barn Swallow has), and its pale yellowish forehead patch. Cliff Swallows are a highly social species and are usually seen in large flocks on their breeding grounds.

Voice: Young birds begin to call early, at five to six days of age, and soon after the calls are recognizable by adults. Cliff Swallows have five call types used selectively for begging for food, sounding the alarm for a predator, courting, nest building, and food-finding. The juvenile begging call changes to a *chur* call when the birds become independent of adults in summer (Brown *et al.*, 2017).

Status: A common summer resident. Its winter range extends from Brazil to Argentina.

Habitats and Ecology: Cliff Swallows nest in large colonies, and a single site may contain hundreds to thousands of nests. In Wyoming they traditionally nest on steep vertical banks near water, but they will also nest beneath bridges and on buildings. The nests are gourdlike structures made of mud that has been gathered and carried back in the bill. The birds' colonial habits, studied extensively by Charles Brown and Mary Bomberger Brown, have led to the evolution of interesting behaviors. For example, the birds brood-parasitize other Cliff Swallow nests by moving eggs from their nest into others, and they can recognize the calls of their own young within a large colony (Brown *et al.*, 2017).

JAN   FEB   MAR   APR   MAY   JUNE   JULY   AUG   SEPT   OCT   NOV   DEC
          xx   xxxx   xxxx   xxxx   xxxx   xxx

House Wren (*Troglodytes aedon*)

Identification: This familiar wren was named for its tendency to nest around houses or in birdhouses. The overall brownish plumage has few field marks, except for a faint superciliary line with some buffy barring on flanks, tail, and wings.

Voice: The House Wren's complex song is a string of intense and boisterous rapidly rising and falling notes. Rendall and Kaluthota (2013) found that one male uttered 194 different song variants. Early in the breeding season, females also utter a much simpler song that sounds like a human squeal (L. S. Johnson, pers. comm.).

Status: A common summer resident, wintering in the southern United States and Mexico.

Habitats and Ecology: Wrens breed in a wide variety of semi-open habitats, especially deciduous woodlands with snags. Natural holes in trees, nest boxes, and a wide variety of other cavities are used for nesting in urban landscapes. House wrens are generally not found in contiguous forests but instead prefer forests thinned by fire, insect defoliation, or human activity (Johnson, 2014). Polygamous mating is typical in this species and was the subject of intensive ornithological research in the Bighorn Mountains region during the 1980s and 1990s (L. S. Johnson, pers. comm.).

JAN	FEB	MAR	APR	MAY	JUNE	JULY	AUG	SEPT	OCT	NOV	DEC
			x	xxxx	xxxx	xxxx	xxxx	xxxx			

American Dipper (*Cinclus mexicanus*)

Identification: The Dipper is North America's only water-dependent songbird. Easily identified, the American Dipper is confined to mountain streams and resembles an overgrown wren but is uniformly gray and has a short cocked tail. The common name "dipper" recalls the species' distinctive bobbing-up-and-down behavior. Other distinguishing features include a blinking white eyelid, and the bird's ability to jump into frigid waters.

Voice: The male's territorial song is loud, melodious, and bubbling, much like a House Wren's.

Status: A common permanent resident.

Habitats and Ecology: This species is found on rapidly flowing mountain streams, often with waterfalls or cascades present. John Muir described their close association as "bird and stream . . . inseparable" (Muir, 1894). Dippers select clear, clean, cold water, and their presence can be used to assess a stream's water quality. Foraging for invertebrates is done by diving underwater, often in rushing streams. Dippers have high-oxygen-carrying blood cells that adapt them to survive in the cold water of mountain streams. Nests are sometimes attached to rock walls or overhangs, or tucked behind waterfalls or under bridges.

JAN	FEB	MAR	APR	MAY	JUNE	JULY	AUG	SEPT	OCT	NOV	DEC
xxxx	xxxx	xxxx	xxxx	xxxx	xxxx	xxxx	xxxx	xxxx	xxxx	xxxx	xxxx

Gray Catbird (*Dumetella carolinensis*)

Identification: This bird was named for its mewing call. It is a grayish bird with a blackish cap and cinnamon under tail-coverts. It is medium-sized with a long tail and often perches holding its tail down.

Voice: Catbirds have a distinctive catlike *meow* call, often uttered with a flick of the tail. The song is a variable mixture of squeaky notes, nasal sounds, and melodious phrases. The Catbird is in the family Mimidae, a group of species that "mimic" the sounds of other birds and will incorporate their songs into its own. Part of this ability is supported by the structure of the syrinx, the organ responsible for song, which allows the Catbird to sing with two voices at the same time. The song repertoire of this species includes more than 100 different song types (Smith *et al.*, 2011), each with a specific pattern of notes.

Status: A common summer resident that winters south along the U.S. Gulf Coast to the Yucatan Peninsula and Central America.

Habitats and Ecology: Catbirds belong to the genus *Dumetella*, which means "small thicket." They prefer dense, moist, deciduous thickets, and the species is commonly found in cottonwood riparian areas. Their favorite habitats are dense shrubs, particularly fruit-bearing shrubs such as native dogwood (*Cornus*), honeysuckle (*Lonicera*), elderberry (*Sambucus*), and plum (*Prunus*).

JAN	FEB	MAR	APR	MAY	JUNE	JULY	AUG	SEPT	OCT	NOV	DEC
				xxx	xxxx	xxxx	xxxx	xxxx			

Sage Thrasher (*Oreoscoptes montanus*)

Identification: The Sage Thrasher is a somewhat elusive thrushlike songbird of sage-brush habitats. In general, this thrasher is a medium-sized songbird with long legs and tail, brownish gray upperparts with two thin white wing-bars, and underparts that are heavily streaked with dark brown spots. The bill is straight, short, and black; the eyes are lemon yellow to amber. Juvenile birds are similar to the adult but are paler and less streaked. The thrasher commonly flicks its tail upward when alarmed (Reynolds *et al.*, 1999).

Voice: Males have a long, continuous warbling song; one male's extended song lasted 22 minutes (Reynolds *et al.*, 1999). The male song can include mimicry and rep-etition of the same notes, often sung from a fencepost. The common call note is a deeper *chuck*.

Status: A common summer resident, wintering in the southern United States to Mexico.

Habitats and Ecology: As the name implies, the Sage Thrasher is tied to the sage-brush steppe and is a sagebrush obligate. The Sage Thrasher requires both dense sagebrush cover for protection and bare ground for feeding and movement as it works the ground for insects. Because of habitat loss, this species has experi-enced a 52 percent population decline between 1966 and 2014 according to the North American Breeding Bird Survey (Sauer *et al.*, 2017). The majority of sage-brush habitats in the west are on public lands and are managed by the Bureau of Land Management; as a result, federal land use policies have a powerful impact on the future of the sagebrush steppe.

JAN	FEB	MAR	APR	MAY	JUNE	JULY	AUG	SEPT	OCT	NOV	DEC
	x	xxxx	xxxx	xxxx	xxxx	xxxx	xxx				

Cedar Waxwing (*Bombycilla cedrorum*)

Identification: "Waxwing" refers to the red tips of the secondary flight feathers, which resemble drops of sealing wax and are present on adults of both sexes. This species closely resembles the commonly overwintering Bohemian Waxwing (*Bombycilla garrulus*) but lacks white wing markings and has gray rather than chestnut under tail-coverts and a breast that is distinctly yellow rather than gray. Adults of both species have a black facial mask; relatively long, pointed wings; and a black tail with a yellow terminal band.

Voice: The most commonly heard vocalization of waxwings is a very high frequency *seee*.

Status: A common permanent resident.

Habitats and Ecology: Open woodlands, primarily of broad-leaved species, are used for nesting, including riparian forests. Locally, areas that have abundant fruiting plants, such as juniper and crabapples, are especially favored, although insects, buds, and other food sources are also consumed. During winter in the Bighorn Mountains region, this highly mobile species joins large, highly social flocks of Bohemian Waxwings in search of persistent berries. Because of their preference for berries and other fruits, waxwings are important dispersers of fruiting plants and ensure the continuity of the habitats on which they depend (Witmer *et al.*, 2014).

JAN	FEB	MAR	APR	MAY	JUNE	JULY	AUG	SEPT	OCT	NOV	DEC
xxxx	xxxx	xxxx	xxxx	xxxx	xxxx	xxxx	xxxx	xxxx	xxxx	xxxx	xxxx

House Finch (*Haemorhous mexicanus*)

Identification: In 1939 a few illegally captured House Finches from western North America were released by the owners of a pet store in New York City to avoid being arrested for selling a protected species. The birds' offspring gradually spread west and within a half-century became one of the most numerous birds in the United States. Males have a red eyebrow and forehead, a brown cap, streaked brown flanks and underparts, and a slightly notched tail. Females and juveniles are streaked with brown overall and lack reddish markings. Males can be distinguished from the similar Cassin's Finch by their smaller beaks, slightly smaller bodies, and the absence of a red crown.

Voice: Males sing a series of short but extended warbling notes ending with an upward or downward slur. Singing sometimes occurs throughout the year, at least in warmer climates. Females sometimes utter a simpler version of the male's song.

Status: An abundant permanent resident, especially near human habitations.

Habitats and Ecology: This species is now generally associated with human habitations over most of its range, but it also uses undisturbed habitats such as grassland and riparian woodlands. Seeds, buds, flowers, leaves, and fruits are preferred foods. It feeds both on the ground and in trees, and commonly visits bird feeders throughout the year.

JAN	FEB	MAR	APR	MAY	JUNE	JULY	AUG	SEPT	OCT	NOV	DEC
xxxx	xxxx	xxxx	xxxx	xxxx	xxxx	xxxx	xxxx	xxxx	xxxx	xxxx	xxxx

Pine Siskin (*Spinus pinus*)

Identification: This rather small (5-inch) finch has a short notched tail, a rather sharp but short beak, and a body that is mostly streaked with brownish and white but also with yellow markings at the base of the tail and on the inner flight feathers. Siskins are usually found in small groups and almost always are associated with conifers or mixed conifer and deciduous forests where they hang upside-down feeding on the end of a conifer branch.

Voice: The Pine Siskin's song is a goldfinch-like series of trills, long down-slurring notes, and rolls. The song also includes short ascending notes like those of the American Goldfinch but are lower and huskier. Their calls include a hoarse *teee* and a hoarse *jeeeah* note.

Status: A common permanent resident whose arrival and departure times are unpredictable.

Habitats and Ecology: Breeding occurs in montane forests, especially high-elevation spruce-fir, cottonwood riparian, and aspen. Their foods are mainly conifer seeds but also include those of aspens. They seasonally feed on sunflowers and insects (Faulkner, 2010). The siskin population is unpredictably irruptive, with its abundance related to variations in seed crops during different years. Siskins can withstand winter temperatures as extreme as –76 degrees F. because of unique metabolic adjustments (Dawson, 2014).

JAN	FEB	MAR	APR	MAY	JUNE	JULY	AUG	SEPT	OCT	NOV	DEC
xxxx	xxxx	xxxx	xxxx	xxxx	xxxx	xxxx	xxxx	xxxx	xxxx	xxxx	xxxx

American Goldfinch (*Spinus tristis*)

Identification: Breeding males have a bright lemon-yellow plumage except for a black forehead and notched tail, and mostly black wings except for white fore-wing patches. Females and winter-plumage males are much duller but have white (males) to pale buffy (females) wing-bars, a short and notched tail, a uniformly yellowish to brownish buff breast, and a short, stubby beak. The species' undulating flight and associated flight call are also diagnostic.

Voice: The social behavior of the American Goldfinch is associated with six distinctive vocalizations which include a *po-ta-to-chip* "contact call" uttered in flight, a "threat call," a *swee-ee* "alarm call," a *tee-yee* "courtship call," a high-frequency "feeding call," and a highly variable song (McGraw and Middleton, 2017). Male display flights in the breeding season are accompanied by song.

Status: A common permanent resident.

Habitats and Ecology: Breeding occurs in deciduous riparian areas, especially where thistles are abundant or cattails are found. The soft "down" of thistles or cattails is used in nest construction, which partly influences their late summer nesting. Also, rather than insects the seeds of thistles and other composite herbs are primarily used to feed the young. Deciduous riparian woodlands near weedy fields provide an ideal nesting situation. During winter the birds range widely over weedy areas and often visit bird feeders that provide thistle seeds or other tiny seeds.

JAN	FEB	MAR	APR	MAY	JUNE	JULY	AUG	SEPT	OCT	NOV	DEC
xxxx	xxxx	xxxx	xxxx	xxxx	xxxx	xxxx	xxxx	xxxx	xxxx	xxxx	xxxx

McCown's Longspur (*Rhynchophanes mccownii*)

Identification: Longspurs are medium-sized birds with long pointed wings and are named for the elongated claw of the hind toe. The facial pattern of a breeding male is striking: a black cap, malar stripe, and breast band, and whitish side of face and throat with a large dark gray or blackish bill. Males have a tail that is mostly white with a T-shaped black pattern produced by central and terminal banding. Females are similar but have no black markings and are gray on the face and throat rather than white with a pinkish bill.

Voice: Longspurs give *larking* flight songs during a parachuting aerial display that consists of a slow descent with outstretched wings and the white-and-black T-patterned tail fanned.

Status: A common summer resident, wintering in the southern United States to Mexico.

Habitat and Ecology: McCown's Longspur is one of the primary grassland endemics restricted to sparsely vegetated native mixed-grass and short-grass prairie with a mixture of herbaceous vegetation (Table 1; Faulkner, 2010). Nests are constructed on the ground next to grasses or shrubs. In Wyoming, the birds are most common in the native grasslands east of Sheridan (Faulkner, 2010) and Ucross. The species has experienced a cumulative decline of 88 percent from 1966 to 2014 and is at risk of becoming threatened or endangered without conservation (Sauer *et al.* 2017; North American Bird Conservation Initiative, 2014).

JAN	FEB	MAR	APR	MAY	JUNE	JULY	AUG	SEPT	OCT	NOV	DEC
	xx	xxxx	xxxx	xxxx	xxxx	xxxx	xxxx	xx			

Spotted Towhee (*Pipilo maculatus*)

Identification: The Spotted Towhee is a large sparrow, easily identified by a black (males) or brown (females) head and breast that resembles a hood, a white-spotted black back, a long white-cornered black tail, and chestnut flanks. The closely related eastern form, the Eastern Towhee (*Pipilo erythrophthalmus*), lacks white back spots. Hybrids that have only slight white back spotting might occasionally occur in eastern Wyoming.

Voice: The male's primary song is a variable version of the Eastern species' *drink-your-tea*. Early in the breeding season, territorial males sing the majority of the daylight hours. The Spotted Towhee's call is a nasal and cat-like *wheee* or *chee-ee*, much like the Eastern species' *tow-eee* call.

Status: A common summer resident, wintering in the southern United States and Mexico.

Habitat and Ecology: Towhees, sparrows, juncos, and buntings are small to medium-sized ground-dwelling birds that are generally brownish and sometimes streaked. They have conical bills for seed eating. Unlike the sparrows, the towhees and the Lark Bunting are brightly colored. Behaviorally, many in this family use both feet simultaneously to scratch for food among litter. Most have complicated and melodious songs, and flight singing is performed by several of the sparrows and the Lark Bunting. Their songs sometimes have an insect-like quality, and some species are known to sing at night. The Spotted Towhee prefers a low, dense, and brushy habitat component with an accumulation of litter and humus, and a protective overhead screen of dense foliage. Towhees often select brushy thickets and canyons where they place their nests on the ground or low in a bush. Towhees are commonly seen on the ground, scratching for insects and seeds in leaf litter (Smith and Greenlaw, 2015).

JAN	FEB	MAR	APR	MAY	JUNE	JULY	AUG	SEPT	OCT	NOV	DEC
			xx	xxxx	xxxx	xxxx	xxxx	xxxx	xx		

Vesper Sparrow (*Pooecetes gramineus*)

Identification: This is the only pale-colored, medium-large grassland sparrow with white outer tail feathers. The adult sexes are alike, with conspicuous whitish eye-rings and a weakly streaked breast that sometimes forms a central spot. Unlike the similar Savannah Sparrow (*Passerculus sandwichensis*) and Song Sparrow (*Melospiza melodia*), the Vesper Sparrow has a paler back, chestnut patches on the upper wing-coverts, and a white-edged tail.

Voice: This species' song is musical and somewhat like that of a Song Sparrow but usually has two pairs of preliminary slurred notes followed by a descending trill: *Here, here; where-where; all together down the hill*. Males often sing in early evening, thus the name Vesper Sparrow.

Status: An abundant summer resident, wintering from the southern United States to Mexico.

Habitats and Ecology: This grassland endemic breeds in dry, open habitats with short vegetation such as native shortgrass and mixed-grass prairie and sagebrush steppe with light to moderate shrub and forb cover (Table 1) where they nest on the ground in a shallow depression. In Wyoming, the availability of sagebrush for nest cover and for song perches is important (Dechant *et al.*, 2000). Males often sing from a high perch, a fencepost, or atop the sagebrush.

JAN	FEB	MAR	APR	MAY	JUNE	JULY	AUG	SEPT	OCT	NOV	DEC
			xx	xxxx	xxxx	xxxx	xxxx	xxxx	xx		

Lark Sparrow (*Chondestes grammacus*)

Identification: This large, long-tailed grassland sparrow has conspicuous white corners on the tail feathers and a very distinctive and contrasting head pattern with bright chestnut ear-patches, a chestnut stripe over the eye, and white and black markings. The breast is unstreaked with a prominent dark breast spot.

Voice: This species was named for the lark-like quality of its song, which is a complex mixture of buzzy notes and trills but typically begins with two loud and clear introductory *twee* notes followed by *twee twee trerere trerere twee twee twee*. Males sing persistently from a high perch, on the ground, or in flight. The call note is a warbler-like *tsip*.

Status: A common summer resident, wintering south to Mexico.

Habitats and Ecology: One of the six passerines endemic to the native grasslands of North America, the Lark Sparrow favors grasslands that have scattered trees, shrubs, and forbs, often selecting transitional habitats between grasslands and forests. Nests are placed on the ground, sometimes at the base of sagebrush or in a tree. During courtship, the male can display with wing drooping and dancing. During migration and in winter, the birds occur in flocks, sometimes joining other sparrows. They can often be seen foraging on the bare ground or in grasses for insects and seeds.

JAN   FEB   MAR   APR   MAY   JUNE   JULY   AUG   SEPT   OCT   NOV   DEC
                              xxxx   xxxx   xxxx   xxxx   xxx

Lark Bunting (*Calamospiza melanocorys*)

Identification: Males are easily identifiable by their black plumage with large white wing-patches evident both in perching and flying birds. Females are also large and heavily streaked with chocolate brown and also have white wing markings and white corners on their tails. Males in winter resemble females.

Voice: Males utter two distinct flight songs, a song given from a perch often used to attract mates, and a more aggressive flight-song produced while flying and most often directed at other males. The songs are a mixture of harsher notes, whistles, and trills (Shane, 2000). The call note is *who-ee-ee* or *hoo-ee*.

Status: A common summer resident, wintering in the southern United States.

Habitats and Ecology: One of the six passerines endemic to the native grasslands of North America, the Lark Bunting favors mixed-grass prairie of moderate density for nesting but also uses shortgrass prairie and sagebrush steppe habitats with a shrub component (Table 1). Lark Buntings exhibit a somewhat colonial nesting behavior, with nests placed only 10 to 15 yards apart. Males typically sing from fenceposts or utter their songs while flying (Dechant *et al.*, 1999, *Lark Bunting*). The birds forage on the ground, and males may follow females as they search for food.

JAN	FEB	MAR	APR	MAY	JUNE	JULY	AUG	SEPT	OCT	NOV	DEC
				xxxx	xxxx	xxxx	xxxx	xxx			

Grasshopper Sparrow (*Ammodramus savannarum*)

Identification: Grasshopper Sparrows are among the smallest and plainest of the grassland sparrows. They appear flat-headed and have a large bill, a plain buffy breast (somewhat striped in juveniles), a pale crown stripe, a short and unmarked tail, and a pale, somewhat yellowish face with contrasting dark eye.

Voice: The Grasshopper Sparrow is one of the few sparrow species in which males and females both sing. The male's song is a grasshopper-like buzzy trill that is used near the nest. Females trill to announce their presence and to attract a mate. The primary male song is often sung from a perch and is a high-pitched note followed by an insect-like *tsick, tsurrrr* (Vickery, 1996).

Status: An uncommon summer resident, wintering south to Mexico.

Habitats and Ecology: A grassland endemic, this sparrow prefers low-elevation mixed-grass prairie with patchy bare ground during breeding season (Table 1; Dechant *et al.*, 1998, *Grasshopper Sparrow*). In Wyoming, they are more commonly found in the native grasslands that extend east from Sheridan and Ucross. True to its name, this species feeds on grasshoppers during the breeding season. They build ground nests of grass, so they are very susceptible to mowing of hayfields from May to July. This sparrow has suffered a significant population decline mainly because of loss of grassland habitats (Sauer *et al.*, 2017).

JAN	FEB	MAR	APR	MAY	JUNE	JULY	AUG	SEPT	OCT	NOV	DEC
				xxxx	xxxx	xxxx	xxxx	xxxx			

Dark-eyed Junco (*Junco hyemalis*)

Identification: This bird is a common and familiar "snowbird" that shows marked geographical variation in plumage coloration that ranges geographically from being mostly black to dark grayish ("slate-colored" race), to having a pearly gray head with a bluish gray cast and pinkish cinnamon flanks ("pink-sided" race). Formerly regarded as consisting of five distinct species, all are now considered a single species collectively named the Dark-eyed Junco (Nolan *et al.*, 2002). The pink-sided race (*mernsi*) is a common breeder in the Bighorn Mountains and the north-central Rockies. The outer tail feathers of all races are white, and the central feathers are blackish, a contrasting pattern that is evident in flight. The pink-sided race is distinguished by the pinkish brown to cinnamon flanks.

Voice: The males' song is a series of musical trills of the same pitch, resembling that of a Chipping Sparrow (*Spizella passerina*).

Status: A common permanent resident. Juncos descend in elevation during winter, when they form foraging flocks at local feeders.

Habitats and Ecology: These sparrows prefer montane forests and aspen groves with a dense understory and plants that provide cover for their ground nests, but they sometimes nest in a small cavity or hole on a mountain rock face (Faulkner, 2010; Nolan *et al.*, 2002). They primarily feed on seeds and insects, scratching on the ground and among underbrush.

JAN	FEB	MAR	APR	MAY	JUNE	JULY	AUG	SEPT	OCT	NOV	DEC
xxxx	xxxx	xxxx	xxxx	xxxx	xxxx	xxxx	xxxx	xxxx	xxxx	xxxx	xxxx

Bobolink (*Dolichonyx oryzivorus*)

Identification: Breeding males have an almost entirely black plumage except for white wing patches, a white rump, and a large patch of yellow on the nape and hindneck. Males appear to be wearing a tuxedo backward. Females closely resemble various female sparrows but are larger and have a buffy crown and eyebrow stripes as well as slightly spotted flanks and a distinctly striped buffy and brown back.

Voice: Male songs are long, contain many notes, and sound like a loud *bob-o-link* described as bubbling. Nine distinct call notes are given mostly during the breeding season: *pink, chunk, buzz, tchenk, whine, quipt, see-yew, zee*, and a begging call (Renfrew *et al.*, 2015).

Status: An uncommon summer resident, wintering in the pampas in southwestern Brazil, Paraguay, and Argentina. Its round-trip, trans-equatorial migration of more than 12,000 miles is one of the longest of all passerine migrations (Renfrew *et al.*, 2015).

Habitats and Ecology: The Bobolink nests in native mixed-grass or tall-grass prairies, wet meadows, hayfields, and grass-sedge fields. The largest breeding concentrations are in northeastern Wyoming along the eastern side of the Bighorn Mountains, and the largest count of 162 birds was in Sheridan in August 1981 (Faulkner, 2010). This species has experienced significant declines throughout its range. The major threats include the loss of grassland habitat, mowing of hayfields during the breeding season, and pesticides.

JAN	FEB	MAR	APR	MAY	JUNE	JULY	AUG	SEPT	OCT	NOV	DEC
				xxxx	xxxx	xxxx	xxxx	xx			

Western Meadowlark (*Sturnella neglecta*)

Identification: Western Meadowlarks are among the most abundant grassland endemic songbirds in eastern Wyoming. Both sexes have bright yellow underparts and a conspicuous black V on the breast region. The upperparts are spotted and striped with brown and buff, and the outer tail feathers are white, a field mark that is apparent only during flight. The nearly identical Eastern Meadowlark (*Sturnella magna*) is extremely rare in Wyoming, but a few have been reported in the eastern counties (Faulkner, 2010).

Voice: The male's flutelike territorial song begins with a series of melodious whistles and descends to a series of rapid gurgling warbles, with much variation in individual song sequences. Singing males often perch on wires or fence posts. Disturbed birds utter a *chupp* call, and fleeing birds emit a harsh rattle (Davis and Lanyon, 2008).

Status: An abundant summer resident, wintering in low numbers along the lower North Platte River in southeastern Wyoming. Most birds migrate to the southern United States and Mexico, but local overwintering sometimes occurs, depending on weather conditions.

Habitats and Ecology: The Western Meadowlark is a secondary endemic species tied to native grasslands. During the breeding season this species occupies open grasslands with thick litter layers of dead grass, including native mixed-grass prairies, low-elevation mountain meadows, pastures, and hayfields (Faulkner, 2010). Early season haying during the nesting period is detrimental to this and many other ground-nesting species.

JAN	FEB	MAR	APR	MAY	JUNE	JULY	AUG	SEPT	OCT	NOV	DEC
		xxxx	xxxx	xxxx	xxxx	xxxx	xxxx	xxxx	xxxx		

Bullock's Oriole, *Icterus bullockii*

Identification: Males of this oriole are not in full color until their second spring, when their orange underparts and black upperparts, plus their large white wing patches and black throats, identify them. Females and first-year males have yellow to pale orange underparts and mostly brown upperparts, with little white on the upper wing feathers. First-year males differ from females in having black throats.

Voice: Like several other icterids, this oriole utters a variety of harsh notes as well as loud whistles, delivered in no particular sequence.

Status: Common summer resident.

Habitats and Ecology: During the breeding season, Bullock's Oriole especially favors river bottom forests of willows and cottonwoods but also occurs in parks and on plains or foothills with aspens, poplars, and similar vegetation. Mature native cottonwoods and landscaping trees provide a major breeding habitat for Bullock's Orioles. During summer, orioles are attracted to the sagebrush along Coal Creek Road near Ucross Ranch. Until a few decades ago, the western Bullock's Oriole was regarded as a species distinct from the eastern Baltimore Oriole (*Icterus galbula*), even though extensive hybridization in the Great Plains then favored the view that they are biologically a single species. However, recent evidence suggests that hybrids are becoming less frequent in the overlap zone, and thus the recognition of two species.

JAN	FEB	MAR	APR	MAY	JUNE	JULY	AUG	SEPT	OCT	NOV	DEC
				xxxx	xxxx	xxxx	xxxx				

Red-winged Blackbird (*Agelaius phoeniceus*)

Identification: Males of this abundant species are entirely black except for their red and yellow shoulders, or epaulets, which are evident on standing as well as flying birds. Immature males are less colorful and are somewhat brown and streaked but with some reddish color on the upper wing. Females are brown and heavily streaked with a yellowish wash around the bill.

Voice: Both males and females have a variety of calls that are used to communicate contact, threat, and distress. Males often sing from a high perch over their territory. The male's song is a loud liquid *kong-ka-ree*, uttered with epaulets raised and the wings partially spread. The predator alarm call of *cheer* is given in response to a raccoon, crow, or hawk (Yasukawa and Searcy, 1995).

Status: This common summer resident sometimes overwinters in towns where there are bird feeders.

Habitats and Ecology: Red-winged Blackbirds breed in wet places like marshes and wetland habitats, where they place their nests low among vertical shoots of the marsh, often in close proximity. They sometimes breed in drier habitats, including hayfields and pasture land. This species is known to join in large mixed flocks with other blackbirds during the nonbreeding season. Large fall roosts of 20,000 birds have been recorded in the Sheridan area (Faulkner, 2010).

JAN	FEB	MAR	APR	MAY	JUNE	JULY	AUG	SEPT	OCT	NOV	DEC
xx	xxxx	xxxx	xxxx	xxxx	xxxx	xxxx	xxxx	xxxx	xxxx	xxxx	xx

Common Grackle (*Quiscalus quiscula*)

Identification: This is a large blackbird with long legs and a long tail. It has pale yellow eyes with a black and highly iridescent plumage. The birds have a glossy purplish blue sheen on the head, neck, and breast that contrasts with their bronze-iridescent bodies. Females are less glossy and smaller. Males and females both have a long and tapering beak with a slight downward curve. Both have a long keel-shaped tail that is often bent upward in a V (males) or U (females) while in flight.

Voice: The male has a loud, wheezy call in spring often described as sounding like a rusty gate or *readle-eak*.

Status: A common summer resident, wintering in the southern United States.

Habitats and Ecology: Grackles are semicolonial in nesting and prefer breeding habitats of cottonwood riparian areas, woody shorelines around lakes, and wooded urban settings where they typically place their nest high in a conifer tree, though they often select birdhouses, woodpecker holes, barns, and occupied bird nests. Their diet varies from insects to fish, mice, and other birds. Grackles are common to abundant in the eastern half of the state, yet they were once considered rare in Wyoming. They continued a major expansion in the early 1970s, and upward of 8,000 birds were observed roosting in Sheridan in the fall of 1979 (Faulkner, 2010).

JAN	FEB	MAR	APR	MAY	JUNE	JULY	AUG	SEPT	OCT	NOV	DEC
		xx	xxxx	xxxx	xxxx	xxxx	xxxx	xxxx	xxx		

Yellow Warbler (*Setophaga petechia*)

Identification: This species is the most uniformly bright yellow of all the North American warblers, and it has a special fondness for foraging in willows (*Salix* spp.). Breeding males have a series of reddish brown breast streaks, while females are generally duller but overall maintain the buttery yellow tones and the prominent black eye.

Voice: The species' song is a distinctive *tseet-tseet-tseet-sitta-sitta-see* or *sweet, sweet, sweet—oh so sweet.*

Status: A common summer resident, the Yellow Warbler winters southward to Central and South America where it feeds in mangrove forests.

Habitats and Ecology: This warbler is one of the most widespread of all warblers. Yellow Warblers prefer moist habitats such as riparian woodlands of aspen and brushy, wet, deciduous thickets, with a preference for willow stands, hawthorn, and honeysuckle. They forage for insects with quick bursts along branches, sometimes singing from high perches. Nests are built in the forks of bushes or trees. Brown-headed Cowbirds (*Molothrus ater*) are frequent brood parasites, laying their eggs in newly started clutches, although the warblers may retaliate by roofing over a parasitized nest and beginning a new clutch (Johnsgard, 1997). Yellow warblers are one of the most common warblers, but their populations have been slowly declining (Sauer *et al.*, 2017).

JAN	FEB	MAR	APR	MAY	JUNE	JULY	AUG	SEPT	OCT	NOV	DEC
				xxxx	xxxx	xxxx	xxxx	xxxx			

Yellow-rumped Warbler (*Setophaga coronata*)

Identification: Formerly considered two species—the Myrtle (*S. c. coronata*) in eastern North America and the Audubon's (*S. c. auduboni*) in the American West—this now single species is named for its conspicuous yellow rump. Males of *auduboni* have a distinctive combination of yellow rump, flank patch, crown, and throat but otherwise are mostly bluish gray above and white below. Females also have yellow rumps and flank markings but otherwise are rather dull in color. Males of *coronata* are similar to *auduboni*, but their throat color is white rather than yellow.

Voice: The male song is a soft, slow warble with even pitch that may rise or fall slightly as it ends. The two main calls are a sharp *chek* or a soft *psit* or *tsee* in flight, which differ between the races.

Status: A common summer resident, the Yellow-rumped Warbler is rare or absent in winter, when the birds migrate south to the southern United States or Mexico.

Habitats and Ecology: This species breeds predominantly in mature coniferous forests and mixed coniferous-deciduous habitats, and occurs at all elevations in the region. It selects conifer trees for nesting and forages from low branches to the highest crown levels. The birds are often seen fluttering out from a tree to catch insects. On migration and during winter, they eat fruits and berries that, among warblers, they are notably able to digest. This adaptation allows them to winter farther north than nearly all other North American warblers (Hunt and Flaspohler, 1998).

JAN	FEB	MAR	APR	MAY	JUNE	JULY	AUG	SEPT	OCT	NOV	DEC
			xx	xxxx	xxxx	xxxx	xxxx	xxxx	xxx		

Western Tanager (*Piranga ludoviciana*)

Identification: Some say seeing a Western Tanager is like looking at a flame: the male of this attractive western songbird during the spring and summer is lemon yellow with coal-black wings, back, and tail and an orange-red head. The female is much duller, mostly yellow below with a greenish yellow back and a black tail and wings, the latter crossed by two white wing-bars. Tanagers are heavier-bodied than warblers and have a short, thick-based bill.

Voice: The male's song is like that of the American Robin but sounds hoarse and consists of two- and three-syllable notes, a *pra-deep*. Because the bird is often inconspicuous in its preferred position in tree canopies foraging for insects, its song is useful for field identification.

Status: This common summer resident winters from Mexico to Costa Rica.

Habitats and Ecology: During breeding, the Western Tanager ranges farther north than other tanagers—as far as northern Canada, where it breeds in open and mixed coniferous and deciduous forests and riparian woodlands. It is common in low- to mid-elevation forests, where it forages on insects and fruits such as wild cherries, elderberries, and serviceberries (Hudon, 1999). This species prefers forests of Douglas fir, ponderosa pine, and lodgepole pine, all of which are present in the Bighorn Mountains region.

JAN	FEB	MAR	APR	MAY	JUNE	JULY	AUG	SEPT	OCT	NOV	DEC
				xxx	xxxx	xxxx	xxxx	xxx			

Bird Checklist for the Ucross Ranch

These 158 species include the abundant to rare birds of the region. Their taxonomy is in accordance with the 2017 taxonomy of the American Ornithologists' Union.

Status

Regional abundance: A = Abundant, C = Common, U = Uncommon, R = Rare

Seasonal occurrence: PR = Permanent Resident, SR = Summer Resident, M = Migrant, WM = Winter Migrant

Habitat

R = Riparian, W = Water, G = Grasslands, S = Sagebrush, U = Urban

Species	Status	Habitat
☐ Canada Goose	A, PR; WM	W
☐ Wood Duck	U, SR	W
☐ Gadwall	C, SR	W
☐ American Wigeon	C, SR	W
☐ Mallard	A, PR	W
☐ Blue-winged Teal	C, SR	W
☐ Cinnamon Teal	U, SR	W
☐ Northern Shoveler	C, SR	W
☐ Northern Pintail	C, SR	W
☐ Green-winged Teal	C, PR	W
☐ Canvasback	U, SR	W
☐ Redhead	U, SR	W
☐ Lesser Scaup	U, SR	W
☐ Common Goldeneye	C, WM	W
☐ Common Merganser	C, PR	W
☐ Ruddy Duck	C, SR	W
☐ Gray Partridge	U, PR	G
☐ Ring-necked Pheasant	C, PR	G
☐ Greater Sage-Grouse	C, PR	G, S
☐ Sharp-tailed Grouse	U, PR	G
☐ Wild Turkey	C, PR	R
☐ Pied-billed Grebe	U, SR	W
☐ Eared Grebe	U, SR	W
☐ Western Grebe	R, SR	W
☐ Clark's Grebe	R, SR	W
☐ Rock Pigeon	C, PR	U
☐ Eurasian Collared-Dove	U, PR	U
☐ Mourning Dove	C, SR	R, G, U
☐ Common Nighthawk	C, SR	G
☐ Common Poorwill	C, SR	G, S
☐ White-throated Swift	U, SR	G
☐ Calliope Hummingbird	U, SR	R, U
☐ Broad-tailed Hummingbird	U, SR	R, U

Species	Status	Habitat
☐ Sora	U, SR	W
☐ American Coot	C, SR	W
☐ Sandhill Crane	C, SR	R, W, G
☐ American Avocet	C, SR	W
☐ Killdeer	C, SR	G, W
☐ Mountain Plover	R, SR	G
☐ Upland Sandpiper	U, SR	G
☐ Long-billed Curlew	U, SR	G
☐ Wilson's Snipe	U, SR	W, R
☐ Spotted Sandpiper	C, SR	R, W
☐ Wilson's Phalarope	C, SR	W
☐ Double-crested Cormorant	C, SR	W
☐ American White Pelican	C, SR	W
☐ Great Blue Heron	C, PR	W
☐ American Bittern	R, SR	W
☐ Turkey Vulture	C, SR	G
☐ Osprey	C, SR	R, W
☐ Bald Eagle	U, SR; C, WM	R, W
☐ Northern Harrier	U, PR	G, W
☐ Swainson's Hawk	C, SR	G
☐ Red-tailed Hawk	C, SR; C, M	R, G
☐ Ferruginous Hawk	U, PR	G
☐ Rough-legged Hawk	C, WM	G
☐ Golden Eagle	U, PR	G, R
☐ Barn Owl	R, SR	G
☐ Eastern Screech-Owl	U, PR	R, U
☐ Great Horned Owl	C, PR	R, U
☐ Burrowing Owl	U, SR	G
☐ Long-eared Owl	U, PR	R
☐ Short-eared Owl	U, PR	G
☐ Belted Kingfisher	C, PR	W, R
☐ Lewis's Woodpecker	U, SR	R
☐ Red-headed Woodpecker	U, SR	R

Bird Checklist for the Ucross Ranch

Species	Status	Habitat	Species	Status	Habitat
☐ Red-naped Sapsucker	U, SR	R	☐ House Sparrow	A, PR	U
☐ Downy Woodpecker	C, PR	R	☐ American Pipit	R, SR	G
☐ Northern Flicker	C, PR	R, U	☐ Gray-crowned		
☐ American Kestrel	C, SR	G	Rosy-Finch	C, WR	G
☐ Merlin	U, PR	G	☐ House Finch	A, PR	U
☐ Prairie Falcon	U, PR	G	☐ Common Redpoll	R, WR	G
☐ Western Wood-Pewee	C, SR	R, U	☐ Pine Siskin	C, PR	R, U
☐ Willow Flycatcher	U, SR	R	☐ American Goldfinch	C, PR	R, G, U
☐ Least Flycatcher	C, SR	R	☐ Evening Grosbeak	U, PR	R
☐ Say's Phoebe	C, SR	G, U	☐ McCown's Longspur	C, SR	G
☐ Cassin's Kingbird	U, SR	G	☐ Lapland Longspur	U, WR	G
☐ Western Kingbird	C, SR	G	☐ Chestnut-collared		
☐ Eastern Kingbird	C, SR	G, R	Longspur	R, SR	G
☐ Dusky Flycatcher	U, SR	R	☐ Snow Bunting	R, WR	G
☐ Loggerhead Shrike	U, SR	G	☐ Green-tailed Towhee	C, SR	S
☐ Northern Shrike	U, WM	G, U	☐ Spotted Towhee	C, SR	R, S
☐ Warbling Vireo	C, SR	R, U	☐ American Tree Sparrow	C, WM	R, G, U
☐ Red-eyed Vireo	C, SR	R, U	☐ Chipping Sparrow	C, SR	R, N, U
☐ Blue Jay	U, PR	G, U, R	☐ Brewer's Sparrow	C, SR	S
☐ Black-billed Magpie	C, PR	R, G	☐ Vesper Sparrow	C, SR	G
☐ American Crow	C, PR	R, G	☐ Lark Sparrow	C, SR	G
☐ Common Raven	U, PR	G, U	☐ Sage Sparrow	U, SR	S
☐ Horned Lark	C, PR	G	☐ Lark Bunting	C, SR	G
☐ Tree Swallow	C, SR	R, W	☐ Savannah Sparrow	U, SR	G, W, R
☐ Violet-Green Swallow	U, SR	R	☐ Grasshopper Sparrow	U, SR	G
☐ N. Rough-winged			☐ Song Sparrow	C, PR	R, W
Swallow	C, SR	R, W	☐ White-crowned Sparrow	R, SR	R
☐ Bank Swallow	U, SR	R, W	☐ Dark-eyed Junco	C, PR; C, WM	G
☐ Cliff Swallow	C, SR	W, U	☐ Yellow-breasted Chat	U, SR	R, W
☐ Barn Swallow	C, SR	W, U	☐ Bobolink	U, SR	G
☐ Black-capped Chickadee	C, PR	R	☐ Red-winged Blackbird	C, SR; C, M	W
☐ Red-breasted Nuthatch	U, PR	R, U	☐ Western Meadowlark	A, SR	G
☐ Canyon Wren	R, PR	S	☐ Yellow-headed Blackbird	U, SR	W
☐ Brown Creeper	U, PR	U	☐ Brewer's Blackbird	C, SR	G, U
☐ Rock Wren	U, SR	G	☐ Common Grackle	C, SR	R, U
☐ House Wren	C, SR	R, U	☐ Brown-headed Cowbird	C, SR	R, G
☐ American Dipper	C, PR	R, W	☐ Orchard Oriole	R, SR	R, U
☐ Ruby-crowned Kinglet	C, SR	U	☐ Bullock's Oriole	C, SR	R, U
☐ Mountain Bluebird	U, SR	G, U	☐ Orange-crowned		
☐ Veery	R, SR	R	Warbler	U, SR	R
☐ Swainson's Thrush	R, SR	R	☐ Yellow Warbler	C, SR	R
☐ American Robin	A, PR	R, U	☐ Yellow-rumped Warbler	C, SR	R
☐ Gray Catbird	C, SR	R	☐ Common Yellowthroat	U, SR	R, W
☐ Sage Thrasher	C, SR	S	☐ Western Tanager	C, SR	R
☐ Brown Thrasher	U, SR	R	☐ Black-headed Grosbeak	U, SR	U, R
☐ European Starling	A, PR	U	☐ Lazuli Bunting	U, SR	R
☐ Bohemian Waxwing	C, WM	R, U	☐ Dickcissel	R, SR	G
☐ Cedar Waxwing	C, PR	R, U			

Appendix

Table 1. Microhabitat characteristics of grass and forb cover utilized by selected grassland bird species

Species	Grass cover	Forb cover
Ferruginous Hawk	Open, short, sparse; prairie dog towns	Light
McCown's Longspur	Open, short, sparse	Moderate
Dickcissel	Dense	Heavy
Grasshopper Sparrow	Sparse to moderate	Light to moderate
Vesper Sparrow	Short, sparse, patchy	Light to moderate
Lark Bunting	Moderate	Moderate with shrubs

From Johnson *et al.*, 1998

Documentation of Rare Species

Please submit to the Bighorn Audubon Society sightings of any species not on this list. A photograph and documentation that includes the date, habitat, and detailed description would be appreciated. Please email bighornaudubon@gmail.com

References

General

Note: Some of the basic biological information in the species profiles is derived from the online Birds of North America (Cornell Lab of Ornithology) and Northern Prairie Wildlife Research Center as well as from the books Johnsgard (1986), Baicich and Harrison (1997), Alderfer (2006), and Faulkner (2010).

Alderfer, J. 2006. *National Geographic Complete Birds of North America*. Washington, DC: National Geographic Society.

Baicich, P. J., and C. J. O. Harrison. 1997. *A Guide to the Nests, Eggs, and Nestlings of North American Birds*. San Diego: Academic Press.

Beetle, A. A., and K. L. Johnson. 1982. "Sagebrush in Wyoming." *University of Wyoming Agricultural Experiment Station Bulletin 779*. Laramie, WY. 68 pp.

Canterbury, J. L. 2018. *Bird Checklist for the Ucross Ranch*. Ucross, WY: Ucross Foundation.

Canterbury, J. L., and P. A. Johnsgard. 2017. *Common Birds of The Brinton Museum and Bighorn Mountains Foothills*. Lincoln, NE: Zea Books. 67 pp. http://digitalcommons.unl.edu/zeabook/57/

Canterbury, J., A. Downing, and P. Lecholat. 2016. *Bird Checklist for The Brinton Museum*. Big Horn, WY: The Brinton Museum.

Canterbury, J. L., P. A. Johnsgard, and H. F. Downing. 2013. *Birds and Birding in Wyoming's Bighorn Mountains Region*. 260 pp. Lincoln, NE: Zea Books. http://digitalcommons.unl.edu/zeabook/18

Downing, H. (ed.). 1990. *Birds of North-Central Wyoming and the Bighorn National Forest*. Sheridan, WY: published by author. 98 pp.

Faulkner, D. W. 2010. *Birds of Wyoming*. Greenwood Village, CO: Roberts and Company. 404 pp.

Fitzgerald, J. A., D. N. Pashley, and B. Pardo. 1999. *Partners in Flight Bird Conservation Plan for the Northern Mixed-Grass Prairie*. Technical Report. Jefferson City, MO: American Bird Conservancy. Version 1.0. 69 pp.

Johnsgard, P. A. 1975. *Waterfowl of North America*. Bloomington: Indiana University Press, 573 pp. (Revised edition, 2010, Lincoln, NE: Zea Books, http://digitalcommons.unl.edu/biosciwaterfowlna/1/)

Johnsgard, P. A. 1981. *The Plovers, Sandpipers, and Snipes of the World*. Lincoln: University of Nebraska Press. 492 pp.

Johnsgard, P. A. 1986. *Birds of the Rocky Mountains with Particular Reference to National Parks in the Northern Rocky Mountain Region*. Boulder: Colorado Associated University Press. 504 pp. (Revised edition, 2009, Lincoln, NE: Zea Books, http://digitalcommons.unl.edu/bioscibirdsrockymtns/1/)

Johnsgard, P. A. 1990. *Hawks, Eagles, and Falcons of North America: Biology and Natural History*. Washington, DC: Smithsonian Institution Press. 403 pp.

References

Johnsgard, P. A. 1993. *Cormorants, Darters, and Pelicans of the World*. Washington, DC: Smithsonian Institution Press. 445 pp.

Johnsgard, P. A. 1997. *The Avian Brood Parasites: Deception at the Nest*. New York: Oxford University Press. 409 pp.

Johnsgard, P. A. 2001. *Prairie Birds: Fragile Splendor in the Great Plains*. Lawrence: University Press of Kansas. 331 pp.

Johnsgard, P. A. 2002. *Grassland Grouse and Their Conservation*. Washington, DC: Smithsonian Institution Press. 157 pp.

Johnsgard, P. A. 2005. *Prairie Dog Empire: A Saga of the Shortgrass Prairie*. Lincoln: University of Nebraska Press. 142 pp.

Johnsgard, P. A. 2009. *Four Decades of Christmas Bird Counts in the Great Plains: Ornithological Evidence of a Changing Climate*. University of Nebraska–Lincoln Digital Commons. 334 pp. http://digitalcommons.unl.edu/biosciornithology/46/

Johnsgard, P. A. 2015. *A Chorus of Cranes. The Cranes of North America and the World*. Boulder: University Press of Colorado. 242 pp.

Johnsgard, P. A. 2019. *A Naturalist's Guide to the Great Plains: Sites, Species, and Spectacles*. Lincoln, NE: Zea Books. http://digitalcommons.unl.edu/zeabook/63/

Johnsgard, P. A., and M. Carbonell. 1996. *Ruddy Ducks and Other Stifftails: Their Behavior and Biology*. Norman: University of Oklahoma Press. 291 pp.

Johnson, D. H., L. D. Igl, J. A. Dechant, M. L. Sondreal, C. M. Goldade, M. P. Nenneman, and B. R. Euliss. 1998. *Effects of Management Practices on Grassland Birds*. Northern Prairie Wildlife Research Center, Jamestown, ND. http://www.npwrc.usgs.gov/resource/literatr/grasbird/grasbird.htm (version 2 July 1998).

Knight, D. H. 1994. *Mountains and Plains: The Ecology of Wyoming Landscapes*. 2nd ed. New Haven, CT: Yale University Press.

Knopf, F. L. 1994. "Avian Assemblages on Altered Grasslands." In *A Century of Avifaunal Change in Western North America*, edited by J. R. Jehl, Jr. and N. K. Johnson, 247–257. *Studies in Avian Biology* 15.

Lindsey, N. 2014. *Wildlife at Ucross*. Privately printed. 3 pp.

Mengel, R. M. 1970. "The North American Central Plains as an Isolating Agent in Bird Speciation." In *Pleistocene and Recent Environments of the Central Great Plains*, edited by W. Dort, Jr. and J. K. Jones, Jr., 280–340. Lawrence: University Press of Kansas.

Montgomery, G. L. 1996. *Riparian Areas: Reservoirs of Diversity*. US Natural Resources Conservation Service Working Paper No. 13. Lincoln, NE: Northern Plains Regional Office.

Muir, J. 1894. *The Mountains of Colorado*. New York: Century.

North American Bird Conservation Initiative. 2014. *The State of the Birds 2014 Report*. US Department of Interior, Washington, DC, USA.

Northeast Wyoming Sage-Grouse Working Group. 2014. *The Northeast Wyoming Sage-Grouse Conservation Plan Addendum*. US Fish and Wildlife Service Partners for Fish and Wildlife Program, Mountain-Prairie Region Strategic Plan, 2017–2021.

References

Opar, Alisa. 2015. "Unprecedented Conservation Efforts Keep Greater Sage-Grouse Off Endangered Species List." Audubon. https://www.audubon.org/news/unprecedented-conservation-efforts-keep-greater-sage-grouse-endangered-species

Paige, C., and S. A. Ritter. 1999. *Birds in a Sagebrush Sea: Managing Sagebrush Habitats for Bird Communities*. Partners in Flight, Western Working Group, Boise, ID. https://ir.library.oregonstate.edu/concern/technical_reports/cv43p2675

Pitkin, M., and L. Quattrini. 2010. *Pocket Guide to Sagebrush Birds*. Petaluma, CA: Rocky Mountain Bird Observatory and PRBO Conservation Science. 70 pp.

Rendall, D., and C. D. Kaluthota. 2013. Song organization and variability in Northern House Wrens (*Troglodytes aedon parkmanii*) in western Canada. *The Auk: Ornithological Advances* 130 (4): 617–628.

Rosenberg, K. V. 2004. *Partners in Flight Continental Priorities and Objectives Defined at the State and Bird Conservation Region Levels*. Ithaca, NY: Partners in Flight and Cornell Lab of Ornithology. 33 pp.

Rowland, M. M., M. Leu, S. P. Finn, S. Hanser, L. H. Suring, J. M. Boyd, C. W. Meinke, S. T. Knick, and M. J. Wisdom. 2005. "Assessment of Threats to Sagebrush Habitats and Associated Species of Concern in the Wyoming Basins." Version 1.1, June 2005. Unpublished report on file at USGS Biological Resources Discipline, Snake River Field Station, 970 Lusk St., Boise, ID 83706.

Sauer, J. R., D. K. Niven, J. E. Hines, D. J. Ziolkowski, Jr., K. L. Pardieck, J. E. Fallon, and W. A. Link. 2017. *The North American Breeding Bird Survey, Results and Analysis 1966–2017*. Version 2.07.2017. USGS Patuxent Wildlife Research Center, Laurel, MD. https://www.mbr-pwrc.usgs.gov/bbs/

Sullivan, B. L., C. L. Wood, M. J. Iliff, R. E. Bonney, D. Fink, and S. Kelling. 2009. eBird: A citizen-based bird observation network in the biological sciences. *Biological Conservation* 142 (10): 2282–2292.

US Fish and Wildlife Service. 2015. Greater Sage-Grouse—Status Review. https://www.fws.gov/greatersagegrouse/status.php

Vickery, P. D., P. L. Tubaro, C. da Silva, B. G. Peterson, J. R. Herkert, and R. B. Cavalcanti. 1999. "Introduction: Conservation of Grassland Birds in the Western Hemisphere." In *Ecology and Conservation of Grassland Birds of the Western Hemisphere*, edited by P. D. Vickery and J. R. Herkert, 2–26. *Studies in Avian Biology* 19.

Wyoming Interagency Vegetation Committee. 2002. *Wyoming Guidelines for Managing Sagebrush Communities with Emphasis on Fire Management*. Wyoming Game and Fish Department and US Department of the Interior, Bureau of Land Management, Wyoming Office, Cheyenne, WY.

The Birds of North America Online References

The Birds of North America project is a multiauthor and joint publication effort begun in the early 1990s by the American Ornithologists' Union (AOU) and the Academy of Natural Sciences, Philadelphia, to monograph all the species of birds known to have bred within the boundaries of the United States and Canada. Individual species accounts (sometimes updated) are available online through the Cornell Lab of Ornithology, Ithaca, New York, on its website https://birdsna.org. The following accounts are cited in this book.

Beason, R. C. 1995. Horned Lark.

Bechard, M. J., and T. R. Swem. 2002. Rough-legged Hawk.

Brown, C. R., M. B. Brown, P. Pyle, and M. A. Patten. 2017. Cliff Swallow.

Colwell, M. A., and J. R. Jehl, Jr. 1994. Wilson's Phalarope.

Davis, S. K., and W. E. Lanyon. 2008. Western Meadowlark.

Dawson, W. R. 2014. Pine Siskin.

Gamble, L. R., and T. M. Bergin. 2012. Western Kingbird.

Gerber, B. D., J. F. Dwyer, S. A. Nesbitt, R. C. Drewien, C. D. Littlefield, T. C. Tacha, and P. A. Vohs. 2014. Sandhill Crane.

Giudice, J. H., and J. T. Ratti. 2001. Ring-necked Pheasant.

Hudon, J. 1999. Western Tanager.

Hunt, P. D., and D. J. Flaspohler. 1998. Yellow-rumped Warbler.

Johnson, L. S. 2014. House Wren.

McGraw, K. J., and A. L. Middleton. 2017. American Goldfinch.

Nolan, Jr., V., E. D. Ketterson, D. A. Cristol, C. M. Rogers, E. D. Clotfelter, R. C. Titus, S. J. Schoech, and E. Snajdr. 2002. Dark-eyed Junco.

Renfrew, R., A. M. Strong, N. G. Perlut, S. G. Martin, and T. A. Gavin. 2015. Bobolink.

Reynolds, T. D., T. D. Rich, and D. A. Stephens. 1999. Sage Thrasher.

Schukman, J. M., and B. O. Wolf. 1998. Say's Phoebe.

Shane, T. G. 2000. Lark Bunting.

Smith, R. J., M. I. Hatch, D. A. Cimprich, and F. R. Moore. 2011. Gray Catbird.

Smith, S. B., and J. S. Greenlaw. 2015. Spotted Towhee.

Vickery, P. D. 1996. Grasshopper Sparrow.

Wiebe, K. L., and W. S. Moore. 2017. Northern Flicker.

Witmer, M. C., D. J. Mountjoy, and L. Elliot. 2014. Cedar Waxwing.

Yasukawa, K., and W. A. Searcy. 1995. Red-winged Blackbird.

Northern Prairie Wildlife Research Center Online References

The Northern Prairie Wildlife Research Center, Jamestown, North Dakota, began in 1965 and later became the National Biological Service within the US Department of Interior. The center is known for leadership on the biology of waterfowl and grassland birds and produces monographs on the effects of management practices on grassland birds. Species accounts can be found at https://www.npwrc.usgs.gov/ or DigitalCommons@University of Nebraska–Lincoln at http://digitalcommons.unl.edu/usgsnpwrc. The following accounts are cited in this book.

Dechant, J. A., M. F. Dinkins, D. H. Johnson, L. D. Igl, C. M. Goldade, and B. R. Euliss. 2000 (revised 2002). *Effects of Management Practices on Grassland Birds: Vesper Sparrow*. Jamestown, ND: USGS Northern Prairie Wildlife Research Center. http://digitalcommons.unl.edu/usgsnpwrc/117

Dechant, J. A., M. L. Sondreal, D. H. Johnson, L. D. Igl, C. M. Goldade, M. P. Nenneman, and B. R. Euliss. 1998 (revised 2002). *Effects of Management Practices on Grassland Birds: Chestnut-collared Longspur*. Jamestown, ND: USGS Northern Prairie Wildlife Research Center. http://digitalcommons.unl.edu/usgsnpwrc/122/

Dechant, J. A., M. L. Sondreal, D. H. Johnson, L. D. Igl, C. M. Goldade, M. P. Nenneman, and B. R. Euliss. 1998 (revised 2002). *Effects of Management Practices on Grassland Birds: Grasshopper Sparrow*. Jamestown, ND: USGS Northern Prairie Wildlife Research Center. http://digitalcommons.unl.edu/usgsnpwrc/147/

Dechant, J. A., M. L. Sondreal, D. H. Johnson, L. D. Igl, C. M. Goldade, A. L. Zimmerman, and B. R. Euliss. 1999 (revised 2002). *Effects of Management Practices on Grassland Birds: Dickcissel.* Jamestown, ND: USGS Northern Prairie Wildlife Research Center. http://digitalcommons.unl.edu/usgsnpwrc/114/

Dechant, J. A., M. L. Sondreal, D. H. Johnson, L. D. Igl, C. M. Goldade, A. L. Zimmerman, and B. R. Euliss. 1999 (revised 2002). *Effects of Management Practices on Grassland Birds: Ferruginous Hawk.* Jamestown, ND: USGS Northern Prairie Wildlife Research Center. http://digitalcommons.unl.edu/usgsnpwrc/149/

Dechant, J. A., M. L. Sondreal, D. H. Johnson, L. D. Igl, C. M. Goldade, A. L. Zimmerman, and B. R. Euliss. 1999 (revised 2002). *Effects of Management Practices on Grassland Birds: Lark Bunting.* Jamestown, ND: USGS Northern Prairie Wildlife Research Center. http://digitalcommons.unl.edu/usgsnpwrc/146/

Dechant, J. A., M. L. Sondreal, D. H. Johnson, L. D. Igl, C. M. Goldade, A. L. Zimmerman, and B. R. Euliss. 1999 (revised 2002). *Effects of Management Practices on Grassland Birds: Upland Sandpiper*. Jamestown, ND: USGS Northern Prairie Wildlife Research Center. http://digitalcommons.unl.edu/usgsnpwrc/118/

Index to Species

www.ingramcontent.com/pod-product-compliance
Lightning Source LLC
Chambersburg PA
CBHW041303290326
41931CB00032B/5